SKY PHENOMENA

SKY PHENOMENA

A Guide to Naked-eye Observation of the Stars

with sections on poetry in astronomy,

constellation mythology, and the Southern Hemisphere sky

Norman Davidson

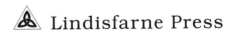 Lindisfarne Press

Published by Lindisfarne Press
RR 4, Box 94 A-1, Hudson, N.Y. 12534

Cover Art: Vincent van Gogh. *The Starry Night.* (1889). Oil on canvas, 29" x 361/4". Collection, The Museum of Modern Art, New York. Acquired through the Lillie P. Bliss Bequest. Photograph © 1993 The Museum of Modern Art, New York.

Grateful acknowledgment is made for the following poems: to the B.J. Brimmer Company for Robert Hillyer's "The Dead Man Ariseth and Singeth A Hymn to the Sun" in *The World's Best Poems*, published by The World Publishing Company, 1946; to F.J. Stephens for the translation of "Invocation" in *Ancient Near Eastern Texts Relating to the Old Testament* by J.B. Pritchard, published by Princeton University Press, 1950; to Faber & Faber, Ltd. for "Stars," "Wanderers," and "Full Moon" by Walter de la Mare in *Collected Rhymes & Verses*, published by Faber & Faber Ltd., 1944; to G.P. Putnam's Sons for "The Ballad of the Northern Lights" by Robert Service in *Ballads of a Cheechako*, published in *Collected Poems* by G.P. Putnam's Sons, 1989; to Holt, Rinehart and Winston, Inc. for "The Star Splitter" in *The Poetry of Robert Frost*, published by Holt, Rinehart and Winston, Inc., 1969 and "Choose Something Like a Star" in *Robert Frost's Poems*, published by Washington Square Press, Pocket Books, 1971; to Macmillan Publishing Co., Inc. for "Moon's Ending" by Sara Teasdale from *Strange Victory* by Sara Teasdale, published by The Macmillan Company, 1933; to The Viking Press, Inc. for "New Moon" by D.H. Lawrence in *The Complete Poems of D. H. Lawrence*, published by The Viking Press, 1964; to Holt, Rinehart and Winston, Inc. for "Star Talk" by Robert Graves in *The Home Book of Modern Verse*, published by Holt, Rinehart and Winston, Inc., 1953; to Patric Dickinson for "Jodrell Bank" by Patric Dickinson in *The World I See*, published by Hogarth Press, Chatto and Windus Ltd., 1960; to Robert Conquest and Hutchinson Ltd. for "For the 1956 Opposition of Mars" by Robert Conquest in *A Book of Science Verse*, published by Macmillan & Co. Ltd., 1961; to Sidney Keyes and Routledge, Chapman & Hall Ltd. for "The Greenwich Observatory" in *The Cruel Solstice* by Sidney Keyes, published by Routledge, 1944; to Rex Raab for "Cosmic Geometry" by Rex Raab in *Looking for Life*, published by The Lanthorn Press, 1983.

Library of Congress Cataloging-in-Publication Data

Davidson, Norman
  Sky phenomena: a guide to naked-eye observation of the stars :
  with sections on poetry in astronomy, constellation mythology,
  and the southern hemisphere sky / by Norman Davidson.
    Includes bibliographical references and index.
    ISBN 0-940262-56-8 (pbk.)
    1. Astronomy—Observers' manuals.   2. Southern sky (Astronomy)
  I. Title.
  QB63.D38 1993   92-43572
  523.8'022'3—dc20   CIP

Cover design: Barbara Richey

10 9 8 7 6 5 4 3 2 1

Printed in the United States of America

To Stephen Sheen,
Waldorf School class teacher,
for his encouragement and patience

Why did not somebody teach me the constellations,
and make me at home in the starry heavens, which are
always overhead, and which I don't half know to this day?

THOMAS CARLYLE (1795–1881)

The deep blue sky was flecked with clouds of a blue deeper than
the fundamental blue of intense cobalt, and others of a clearer
blue, like the blue whiteness of the Milky Way. In the blue depth
the stars were sparkling, greenish, yellow, white, rose, brighter,
flashing more like jewels, than they do at home—even in Paris:
opals you might call them, emeralds, lapis, rubies, sapphires.

VINCENT VAN GOGH (1853–1890)

Contents

Foreword   vii

Introduction   ix

1   The Stars—I   1

2   The Stars—II   13

3   The Sun   23

4   The Moon   42

5   Eclipses   54

6   The Planets   60

7   The Copernican Revolution   66

8   Comets and Meteors   88

9   The Southern Hemisphere Sky   101

10 The Stars in Poetry   117

Appendices

1   Astronomical Events   161

2   Technical Data   167

3   Astronomical Symbols   175

4   Star Maps for Observers at the Equator   177

5   Useful Materials and Publications   179

6   Some Famous Individuals in the History
      of Astronomy   182

7   Glossary of Astronomical Terms   183

Index   193

Sources for "The Stars in Poetry"   201

Foreword

In what passes for a more environmentally conscious age, most of us rarely see or notice the sky, which is pretty much half of the environment no matter how you slice the horizon. Even when by chance we fall under the spell of the waxing crescent Moon dangling in the colors of the sunset, most of us aren't quite sure what it's going to do next. Is it growing? Is it shrinking? When will it appear again? We get questions about this kind of thing every day at Griffith Observatory in Los Angeles. People who have suddenly spotted a "half Moon" call us and want to know what the Moon is doing in the daytime sky.

It's not just the Moon that mystifies us. Our city lights have erased most of the stars from the night sky. Seasons that once were measured by the day-by-day progress of the point of sunrise along the horizon are lost behind urban skylines. Time once measured in the lengths of shadows or height of the Sun is now provided in digital readout. We have lost touch with the sky. We have forgotten how it works. Norman Davidson knows, however, that now and then some of us will be up before the Sun and will catch sight of Venus brilliant in the dawn. Others will be lucky enough to be in the right place at the right time for an eclipse. Despite our estrangement with the sky, it provides never-ending opportunities to revive the bond. So in this book Norman Davidson has made sure we can re-encounter the cyclical and luminous wonders on the celestial dome with some understanding of the patterns and why they occur.

Sky Phenomena—A Guide to Naked-eye Observation of the Stars shows how the sky works—the daily trail of the Sun and nightly travels of stars, the phases and placement of the Moon, the mechanisms of eclipses, the vagrancies of the planets, and more. It's an owner's manual for the sky. And in a bid for hemispheric equity, the author has also given us a detailed account of how all of this looks below the equator, under the Southern Hemisphere's skies.

You don't have to look far to find a solid endorsement for this endeavor. In the rich collection of astronomical excerpts from world literature that comprises Chapter 10, you will find a short and sweet 2500-year-old declaration of the sky's value:

"...take away the firmament, I will be nothing."

In the last hundred years or so, most of that firmament has been taken from us. We are less for our loss of the sky, but Norman Davidson has given us the bootstraps we need to pull ourselves back up to heaven...or at least for a good look at it.

E. C. KRUPP, *Director*
Griffith Observatory, Los Angeles

Introduction

When I was a student in the teacher training course at Emerson College in England, I used to walk about a mile across local farmland to and from class, morning and evening, and could not help coming under the influence of the sky as it changed its face through the seasons. I remember particularly noticing the Moon and wondering what lay behind the alterations in its shape and position. I decided not to look up a book on the subject until I had worked the problem out for myself there and then under the wide Sussex skies. Previously I had certainly had some interest in the stars, but beginning with these field walks, and later after reading my first observational astronomy book from cover to cover,* I developed a love for the sky which has since led me to devote much of my spare time, and professional time, to learning and teaching this fascinating subject. In fact, it led me to write this book in the hope that it may help other people in taking up a conscious study of what is our greater environment—the turning sky.

I say "conscious study" very deliberately, because I discovered that only when I had grasped the laws and principles behind the movements of the stars did there grow in me a deep enthusiasm and desire to observe more. When I found the principles behind the Moon's changing appearance, I longed to experience it again and again, and each waxing crescent in the west in the course of the year was a special event. Every crescent was different in its position and visibility, and the character of each one had to be experienced and confirmed first hand. The Moon became more than a fetching image; it began to speak a seasonal language.

*"The Revolving Heavens" by Reginald Waterfield, which still remains excellent basic reading fifty years after its first publication. He wrote it for the renewed interest in naked-eye astronomy arising in Britain during the Second World War when the lighting blackout revealed the constellations above the cities, and many defense workers on night observation duty had "the stars thrust upon them."

The magic of the subject has to be experienced for oneself, and there is little point in elaborating on that experience in a book like this. If the book were written with such elaborations, it might be interesting literature only for a while and then languish on the shelf. Too much written, secondhand magic tends to replace rather than engender the firsthand experience. I find that the most-thumbed books on this subject are those which contain a good measure of principles and laws as well as descriptions. Certainly, the draft manuscript of this book has become dog-eared enough over the last few years through being passed round among needy school teachers who were beginners in astronomy, yet required lesson material in sky phenomena that children could relate to through their own experience with the naked eye. At one stage I had to rescue the uncorrected draft from a school library where it had been catalogued for borrowing. Although this need of the teacher prompted the manuscript in the first place, its present form makes it suitable for any beginner wanting a guide to basic sky lore.

One problem for the beginner is to find a text that is elementary without being too technical, descriptive without being too sentimental; that sticks to what the normal, unaided eye can see, and covers something approaching the whole spectrum of Earth-centered astronomy. Strangely enough, this is a tall order in the midst of today's information explosion. Many people know through television programs and articles about the Galileo spacecraft mission to Jupiter, for example, but few know where Jupiter is in the sky, what it looks like, or what it will do next against the background of the stars..

Dangers lie in wait for the unsuspecting seeker after a simple written introduction to astronomy. This subject in particular is open to extremes in two directions—either a too-quick plunge into abstract concepts about the universe (inevitably giving rise to fiction-science in the mind of the student), or excessive popularization, reducing it to games and gimmicks. At worst these are put together in the name of capturing, particularly, children's interest. But then the living basis of the subject—the well-informed experience of the sky as we see it—suffers. Yet, paradoxically, the stars are one subject for which children have a natural wonder and receptivity, and if adults start with an experience of the unvarnished laws and beauty of the starry sky, then they can meet the younger generation on its own ground.

The other side of the story I started with about *seeing* the Moon for the first time, is that I was already thirty-six years old and had never been taught astronomy properly at school. The subject is still not a serious part of the curricula of most schools—presumably because it is not "practical" and teachers have not been trained in it. But surely it is practical enough to know about the phenomena of our greater environment and its natural relationship to, and support of, so many other subjects—such as literature, history, mythology, geometry, math, science, geography, or travel. Knowledge of Earth-centered, naked-eye astronomy is vital to, for example, a study of medieval literature. It was the model upon which earlier concepts of the universe were based and is still the model for our immediate experience now. The situation prompted C.S. Lewis to write *The Discarded Image* based on a series of his lectures at Oxford, to try to fill in this educational gap.

Such cosmic support for education is needed far beyond Oxford. The educated person today knows little about the modern sky, far less the medieval one. In 1988 Matthew Schneps of the Harvard-Smithsonian Center for Astrophysics in Cambridge, Massachusetts, directed a half-hour film called *A Private Universe* in which he interviewed about twenty people comprising Harvard seniors, alumni, and faculty at the Harvard graduation ceremony that year. When asked why the Moon appeared in different shapes like crescent or half, most of them said it was because of the Earth's shadow. Again, most were of the opinion that it was hotter in summer than in winter because the Sun was closer to the Earth in summer—an idea not derived from observation and an unlikely mistake for even medieval graduates or professors to have made. Altogether, only about two of the twenty people interviewed answered both questions correctly.

However, there are heartening signs in the educational world. Irwin Shapiro, director of the same Harvard-Smithsonian Center, initiated Project STAR (Science Teaching through its Astronomical Roots), which is now being taught in schools in at least thirteen states in the U.S.A., funded by the National Science Foundation. A special feature of the program is the extended use of three-dimensional models. "To convert from three dimensions to two and back to three again leads to special reasoning ability," it is explained. "Facts are easy; concepts are hard," says Shapiro. A major goal is for STAR students to acquire an improved grasp of basic scientific concepts and mathematics. Another educational support for astronomy in the U.S.A. is the newsletter *The Universe in the Classroom*, which is offered free to teachers and is sponsored by the Astronomical Society of the Pacific, the American

Astronomical Society, the Canadian Astronomical Society, and the International Planetarium Society. Its counterpart in Britain is *Gnomon*, the newsletter of the Association for Astronomy Education, which has a network of resource centers throughout the country.

This book has been written for the beginner or teacher who has little or no prior experience in astronomy. It arises in its own way out of my earlier book *Astronomy and the Imagination* (Arkana/Penguin Books), and students may wish to refer to that to amplify what is presented here. But, as far as the classroom is concerned, no book can be a substitute for the enthusiasm and imagination of the teacher inspiring students to enter the subject fully. The written word is then a framework out of which the spoken word can take flight in the creative teaching moment. Therefore no pedagogical methods are dealt with here which would cramp the instructor's style. Background material is offered in a free way. The teacher must select from it as he or she will, for a particular course.

However, I stand by one aspect of the presentation—the sequence of the topics from chapter to chapter for middle school students. The sequence is organic, from the celestial sphere to circumpolar stars, equatorial stars, Sun, Moon, and so on. It is a development from the whole to the part, an analytical process. One consequence of this is that the Copernican planetary system and heliocentric astronomy are not directly dealt with until after the geocentric phenomena of the planets have been grasped. This is true both psychologically and historically. For older students, say in eleventh or twelfth grade, one could reverse the process and start with a whole comprising completely modern aspects of the subject like cosmology, astrophysics, and the history of space exploration, then work back to a recalling of what every astronomer starts with even if calculating the path of Mars round the Sun—i.e., measurement of the apparent path of Mars round the Earth. Alternatively, short courses in astronomy could be given in each of the four high school grades, concentrating on the Sun in ninth grade, the Moon in tenth, the planets in eleventh, and the stars and cosmology in twelfth. There is, of course, much else to be considered in teaching astronomy that is beyond the scope of this text; for example, the introduction of the telescope in both elementary and high school courses.*

*Hint for elementary school teachers: 10 (magnification) x 50 (aperture) binoculars mounted on a tripod show the moons of Jupiter more or less as Galileo saw them.

The impulse for this text arose out of my teaching experience in Waldorf schools in England and the United States. Waldorf schools were founded by Rudolf Steiner in 1919 and since then have grown to form one of the largest independent school movements in the world, attracting increasing attention with their creative approach to education. Astronomy can be taught in Waldorf schools at any level, but the subject receives proper space twice in the curriculum for the age groups twelve to thirteen and seventeen to eighteen. For the assistance of teachers anywhere, not only in Waldorf schools, I have included some pages on constellation mythology, a chapter of poems and quotations with astronomical themes, and historical items scattered through the text to keep the cultural element close to the subject.

One last word connected with the heartening signs for astronomy in the classroom, and the young person's natural creativity (if left unspoiled) concerning the stars. Not long ago a lecturer (Stephen James O'Meara) spoke about the stars to sixth graders from Maimonides School in Brookline, Massachusetts. Afterward their teacher asked them to create their own constellations and myths. O'Meara says he anticipated stories about astronauts, rocket ships, and extraterrestrials. Instead the children produced stories with imagination, charm, and wit. Here is one of them, by Tzvi Harow:

> Many years ago in ancient Greece, there lived three evil witches who ruled the city. These witches had only one eye and one tooth among themselves—the eye had special powers and the tooth had venom. Many mortals tried to kill these witches. But the witches, who passed the eye and tooth back and forth, always managed to see their rivals and bite them.
>
> One day, a mortal named Danny heard about the witches' powers. Danny, who was well respected in his town for his strength, set off to kill the witches. The journey was long, but once he got there, Danny took out his sword and attacked. Before long, the witches were dead.
>
> Today, we can see the witches passing their eye and tooth in the winter sky. They are the three stars in a row (Orion's Belt) that twinkle at different times.

I wish to record my thanks to those individuals who especially helped me in the preparation of the manuscript for this book: Firstly, Jack Mills, one of my students in the teacher training course at the Waldorf Institute in Spring Valley, New York, an accomplished draftsman, who manfully took on the task, during his summer vacation, of redrawing all of my 180 or so line illustrations. Secondly, Guy Ottewell, creator of the excellent "Astronomical Calendar"—a mine of invaluable star information published each year—who took time out of his busy days to set up computer programs to produce the illustrations of the northern sky views seen from the Southern Hemisphere in Chapter 9. Thirdly, Paul Davis, an amateur astronomer and teacher, whose sharp mind and eye were invaluable in the correcton of the proofs.

Finally, I dedicate Chapter 9, "The Southern Hemisphere Sky," to Hans and Christine Guldemond, who so warmly hosted my wife, Annelies, and me on a visit to Perth, Australia, where we experienced the magnificent Southern skies and saw Halley's Comet high in the Milky Way.

NORMAN DAVIDSON
Spring Valley, New York
January, 1993

Chapter One

The Stars—I

The Celestial Sphere

The impression received on standing under the sky on a clear night is that one is surrounded by a dome or hemisphere of stars. This is the beginning of all astronomy and the phenomenon to which astronomers of all kinds, ancient and modern, must refer back—it is the celestial given. The horizon forms a circle, with the observer at the center (Figure 1).

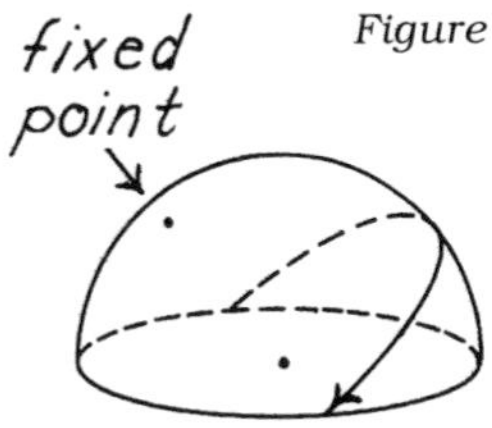

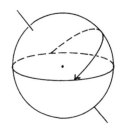

Figure 1

fixed
point

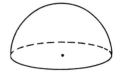

Figure 2

A further observation follows if one remains under the night sky for a length of time. This is that the stars move together. The whole hemisphere appears to turn above one's head. Close observation over a number of hours reveals that the hemisphere turns on a fixed point above the horizon (Figure 2).

This movement shows some stars rising above the horizon and others setting. The impression is thus given of the stars being on a sphere, half of which is hidden, with the observer at the center. The sphere turns on an axis through the fixed point (Figure 3).

Figure 3

The fixed point is called the north celestial pole (seen by observers north of the Earth's equator) and the sphere's axis of rotation passes through it and down to an unseen south celestial pole. For the observer, the direction to the north celestial pole also indicates geographical, or true, north, from which the other cardinal directions are derived (Figure 4).

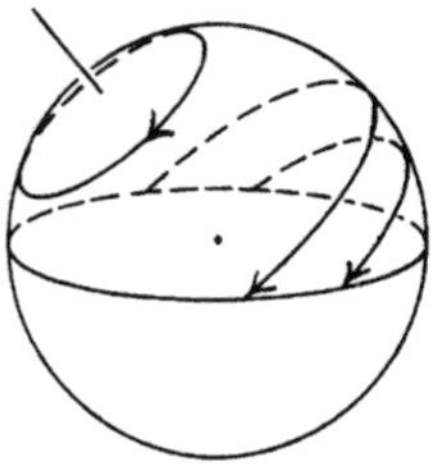

Figure 4

It can now be seen that, while some stars rise and set, others, toward the north, do not (Figure 5). The latter make circles above the horizon and are called circumpolar stars.

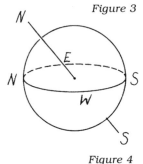

Figure 5

From our position in the center of the sphere, the horizon in any one direction appears level, and can be shown as a straight line. Looking toward the four cardinal points of the compass, the observer sees star movements as in Figures 6, 7, 8, and 9.

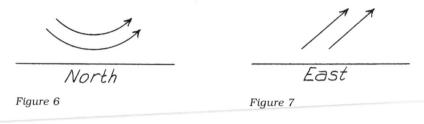

North

Figure 6

East

Figure 7

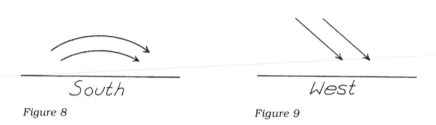

South

Figure 8

West

Figure 9

The easterly and westerly star movements are shown as straight lines since the stars seem to move on lines parallel to each other. For a definition of the curves to north and south, see the Supplementary Exercises at the end of Chapter 2.

The Northern Sky

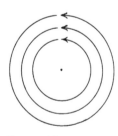

Figure 10

If we lift our gaze above the northern horizon in the direction of the pole, we have the impression of stars turning round the pole anticlockwise in circles (Figure 10), one revolution of each star taking 23 hours 56 minutes. This is called a sidereal (star) day, which is 4 minutes shorter than an ordinary day.

We can now show the movement of one set of these circumpolar stars in the course of a sidereal day. The best known make up the asterism of the Plough (or Big Dipper) in the constellation of the Great Bear. An asterism is a pattern of bright stars within the larger area of a constellation. The Plough has seven stars, as shown in Figure 11. The top star on the right is called Dubhe (meaning bear), and the line through Dubhe and

Merak points toward the pole. The distance from Dubhe to the pole is approximately the same as the distance from Dubhe to the far left star, Alkaid. (All three star names are Arabic.)

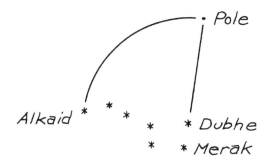

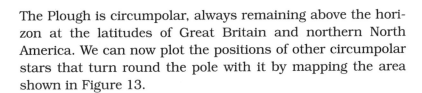

Figure 11

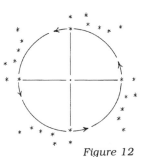

Figure 12

A ruler and compass can thus be used to determine the pole, from which a circle can be drawn through Dubhe. Quarter divisions on the circle give the star's position roughly every six hours. The remaining stars in the asterism can be drawn freehand without turning the page round, as an exercise in symmetry (Figure 12).

The Plough is circumpolar, always remaining above the horizon at the latitudes of Great Britain and northern North America. We can now plot the positions of other circumpolar stars that turn round the pole with it by mapping the area shown in Figure 13.

We will have to imagine that we are standing in the middle of the sphere and that the part of the dome facing us and curving from horizon to overhead and left and right as we face the north celestial pole has been flattened onto the page in Figure 14, with the pole in the middle. With this particular drawing (the stars moving in circles), the horizon cannot be correctly represented geometrically by a straight line and is left out for simplicity.

To make a map, lines of reference are needed. Two sets of circles achieve this, one set with centers on the polar axis and their planes at right angles to it (circles of declination), and the other set passing through both poles (hour circles) as shown in Figure 15.

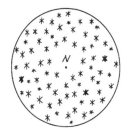

Figure 13

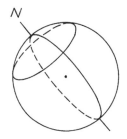

Figure 14

Figure 15

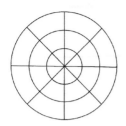

Figure 16

When the northern part of the sphere is flattened on the page, the circles round the polar axis remain circles, but the circles through the poles appear like straight lines (Figure 16). This resembles looking into the inside of an umbrella, and an umbrella with a few sticky-paper stars can be held up and rotated anticlockwise to demonstrate the situation.

We are now ready to map the northern stars and can start with a point in the middle of a page representing the north celestial pole. From this point measure 5 points equal distances apart along a line. Draw circles through these points with the pole as center (Figure 17).

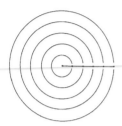

Figure 17

The outer circle should now be divided into 24 equal parts, starting from the line already drawn, and 24 radii drawn to the pole (Figure 18).

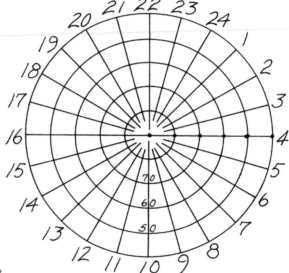

Figure 18

This provides a kind of graph into which we can place the stars in their positions. The radii are numbered 1 to 24, representing hours. The circles and their center indicate intervals of 10, from 40 to 90, representing degrees on the celestial sphere. This wheel, with its radii numbers, turns anticlockwise once in 23 hours 56 minutes. The wheel has been stopped to show the sky at 9 p.m. in early October. We can now plot some prominent circumpolar stars. The names of constellations, within which particular stars and asterisms lie, have been underlined (Figure 19).

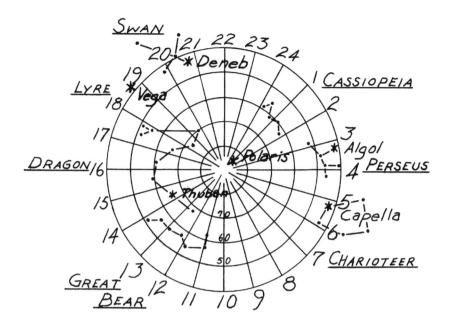

Figure 19

These are some of the main stars in and around the circumpolar region. To show the 9 p.m. positions of these stars at the beginning of other months, the wheel with stars fixed to it has to be drawn after being rotated two hours anticlockwise per month—i.e., number 12 placed at the bottom will be the position for 9 p.m. in early November, 14 for December, 16 for January, 18 for February, 20 for March, 22 for April, 24 for May, 2 for June, 4 for July, 6 for August, and 8 for September. In the course of any one night and day in the year the stars will circle round the pole as in Figure 12, turning one hour angle (indicated by the numbers in Figure 19) every hour.

It should be noted that Polaris is a short distance from the pole and circles round it with the other stars. In fact the pole moves very slowly over hundreds of years, and its closest approach to Polaris will occur on March 24, 2100,* when it will be placed just under the distance of the apparent diameter of the Moon from that star. Polaris is quite faint but is easily detected because it stands relatively alone.

*According to the mathematician/astronomer Jean Meeus (*Journal of the British Astronomical Association*; October, 1990).

Mythology

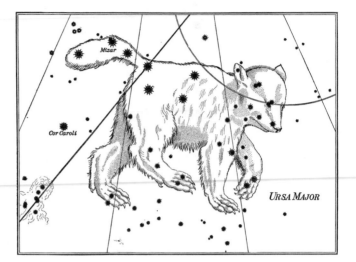

There follow a few brief sketches of old legends connected with the constellations already indicated for the northern sky. The young student can choose a creature, person, or thing mentioned in the stories to draw or paint, and embed the stars of the constellation within it. Such illustrations were frequently made by artists in the past; Plate 1 shows one of them slightly adapted from a drawing by Johann Bayer (1572-1625) depicting the Great Bear (Ursa Major) and its stars, including the asterism of the Plough or Big Dipper.

Polaris, or the POLE STAR, has been used for navigation on sailing ships of the past because of its closeness to the "motionless" pole and its comparatively fixed position in relation to the horizon from any one geographical latitude. Some called it the Lodestar (guiding star). In figurative language, one's lodestar is one's aim or guiding principle. The Finnish people call it Taehti or the Star at the Top of the Heavenly Mountain. In China one name for it was Great Imperial Ruler of Heaven. When the earthly emperor gave certain audiences, he sat on his throne facing south so that the Pole Star was above his head for those he received, and they faced both the heavenly and earthly emperor at once. The Laplanders called the Pole Star the North Nail that held up the heavens. The Arabs called it the Northern Axle or Mill Peg, the sphere of stars around being imagined as a turning millstone. In India the legendary Prince Dhruva who startled the gods by being able to stand motionless on one leg for more than a month, was appointed as the Pole Star round which the stars and planets turn—"like the upright axle of the corn mill circled without end by the laboring oxen." It should be remembered that ancient references to the Pole Star relate to whichever star was nearest to the pole at that time. Polaris is in the constellation of the Little Bear (Ursa Minor).

The image of the oxen turning the millstone of the sky arises in Greek and Latin literature with a description of the seven major stars in the constellation of the GREAT BEAR as seven threshing oxen. However, several different civilizations have also pictured the constellation as a bear. There are various legends, a Greek one relating how Callisto, a nymph and companion of the huntress Artemis, was beloved by the god Zeus. His wife Hera was jealous and he changed the nymph into a she-bear. Hera caused the bear to be killed by Artemis in the hunt and Zeus placed the bear among the stars. The early Teutonic nations knew the constellation as the Wagon, it also being known as the Chariot among the ancient Greeks.

The name Chariot was also given by the Assyrians to the constellation we know today as the CHARIOTEER (Auriga). But the Greeks called it the Holder of the Reins. Capella, the name of its beautiful golden star, means She-Goat—the goat which suckled the infant Jupiter and whose horn Jupiter broke off in his play; the horn became the legendary Horn of Plenty, which was filled with whatever its possessor wished. On illustrated star maps the She-Goat was often depicted being carried on the shoulder of the Chariot Driver.

The constellation PERSEUS is named after the Greek hero who cut off the head of the female monster Medusa, the sight of whose face turned the onlooker to stone. The Arabs, following the legend, called the constellation the Bearer of the Demon's Head, and one of its stars, Algol, was their Demon Star. It was also called the Blinking Demon and in fact is a variable star, meaning that it dims and brightens periodically. Algol does this over a period of about three days during which it dims sharply for a few hours. The original Arab form of the name was ra's al-ghul, from which our word "ghoul" is derived.

The constellation CASSIOPEIA is named after the legendary Greek queen, and the W-shaped asterism is designated as her chair. She is sometimes called "heaven's troubled queen" and the story relates how she, wife of Cepheus, boasted that she was more fair than even the beautiful sea nymphs. The nymphs then arranged it that when the queen was placed among the stars after her death, she sat in a chair which turned upside-down round the pole to teach her humility. The constellation is also famous for a New Star appearing there in 1572, which stayed for about a year and a half and was observed by the famous Danish astronomer Tycho Brahe. It has long been known as Tycho's Star, and flashed out brighter than the planet Venus, taking on a brilliant white color, then later red, before dying away. Its position among the stars of Cassiopeia is shown in Figure 20.

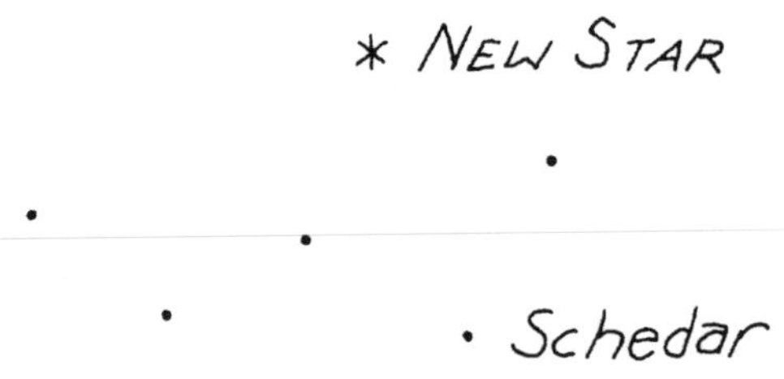

Figure 20

The constellation of the SWAN (Cygnus) has within it the asterism called the Northern Cross which lies inside the Milky Way. This area of the sky around the Swan has long been associated with birds by different ancient peoples. One legend relates that the Swan is the transformed hero Orpheus, who enchanted men, beasts, trees, and rocks with his harp or lyre. In an ancient star list from the Euphrates region, the Swan was called Bird of the Forest. The Arabs called it the Flying Eagle or the Hen, and it was also known as the Hen in early Egypt. The name of the constellation's bright star, Deneb, comes from the Arabic and means tail.

Next to the constellation connected with Orpheus lies LYRA, his lyre, according to one legend—and old Roman coins showed the constellation depicted thus. The ancient Britons called it King Arthur's Harp, and in Bohemia it was the Fiddle in the Sky. But it has also been associated with birds. The name Vega for the constellation's foremost star (which is the brightest in the northern hemisphere of the sky, above the celestial equator) comes from the Arabic meaning Swooping Eagle or Vulture.

The ancient Persians knew the winding constellation of the DRAGON (Draco) as a man-eating serpent, and today we call it Dragon from the Greeks. The latter saw the creature residing within the garden of the Hesperides, or Daughters of the Evening. There, according to one description, the Dragon was guardian of the stars or golden apples which hung from the Pole Tree in the Garden of Darkness. In Egypt the constellation was Typhon or Set, ruler of darkness and the circumpolar stars, and enemy of the Sun. Its main star, Thuban, means Serpent or Dragon in the original Arabic. Around 3000 B.C. Thuban was the Pole Star, caused by the fact that the north celestial pole slowly moves in a circle which passes through the body of the Dragon.* In about A.D. 10,000 it will be the turn of Deneb to be the brightest star nearest the pole, and around A.D. 14,000 it will be Vega (Figure 21).

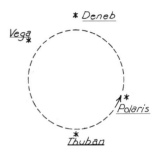

Figure 21

Supplementary Exercises

1.

An interesting and useful project based on the study of circumpolar stars is to make a nocturnal—a medieval instrument used by sailors for telling the time by the stars at night.

First, one requires a handle and disc made of wood, with a hole in the middle of the disc (Figure 22).

Next, a nut and bolt, with a hole through their centers (the bolt to fit through the hole in the wood) so that they hold the disc from either side (Figure 23).

The author has found that the most easily available hollow bolt of this kind is a brass joint for gas pipes, with a half-inch diameter hole.

A paper disc is now pasted onto the wooden one, divided into 12 and marked with the months (Figure 24).

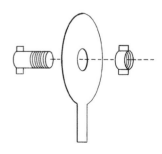

Figure 22

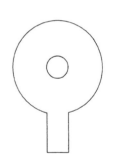

Figure 23

*To draw this circle (of the precession of the pole) on a map like Figure 19, place the point of a pair of compasses at declination 66.5 degrees on hour angle 18 (in Draco for the Northern Hemisphere) and draw a circle through the pole. For the Southern Hemisphere, choose declination -66.5 degrees on hour angle 6 (in Dorado).

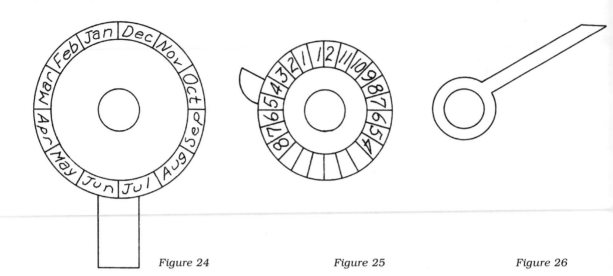

Figure 24   Figure 25   Figure 26

A smaller cardboard disc is then made which will lie on top of the paper disc, being divided into 24 and marked with hours from 8 a.m. through 12 midnight to 4 p.m. The 4:14 a.m. point is extended into a marker, 63.4 degrees from the 12 midnight position (Figure 25).

Lastly, a cardboard pointer is cut which has one edge aligned with the center of the hole, and which is about twice as long as the radius of the wooden disc (Figure 26).

These parts are assembled in the order in which they are described, with the nut and bolt holding the instrument together front and back (Figure 27).

The instrument is now made ready for use by adjusting the marker on the smaller disc to the month and approximate date on the larger disc. The nocturnal is held, handle downward, so that the Pole Star can be seen through the central hole, the plane of the disc being perpendicular to the line of sight. The pointer is moved until it lines up with the "pointer" stars of the Plough (Big Dipper)—as in Figure 28.

The positioning in Figure 27 indicates about 9:30 p.m. in the middle of February. Finer accuracy can be obtained by grading the months in terms of days and the hours in terms of minutes.

As an indoor exercise, reverse the procedure and determine the position in the sky of the Plough at a particular time and date.

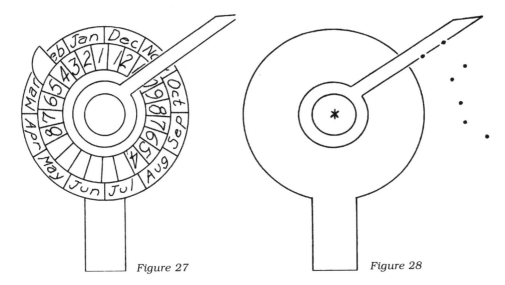

Figure 27

Figure 28

2.

A simpler version of the nocturnal for younger children is a star clock made from two circular pieces of cardboard. One piece is divided into twelve equal parts round the edge, each division representing one month, the months ordered clockwise. Hours are then marked anticlockwise at 24 division intervals, with midnight (24 hours) at the border line between December and January (Figure 29).

A second cardboard disc smaller than the first, not covering the hour numbers, is placed on top of the first disc. A "time" arrow is marked anywhere on its circumference, then a line from the center marked 63.4 degrees clockwise from it. This line relates to the two "pointer stars" of the Plough (Figure 30).

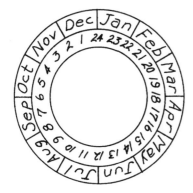

Figure 29

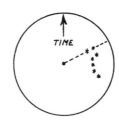

Figure 30

Holes can be put through the centers of the discs and a split pin inserted to hold them together. Facing the North Star, the discs should be held up in front of it like the first nocturnal, with the date at the top and the "pointer" line directed to the Plough's pointer stars. The arrow will then indicate the time. As with the nocturnal, this instrument can be used in the classroom to find where the Plough is at any moment, by setting the dials to the correct date and time.

3.

The stars in Figure 19 can be plotted on a disc of thin cardboard. Prick holes through the cardboard at the stars' positions and place the disc against a window pane. The stars will shine through as points of light.

Chapter Two

The Stars—II

The Zodiac

As explained in Chapter 1, the stars on the celestial sphere to the south of the circumpolar stars rise and set. The best way to demonstrate this part of the sky is to use a celestial globe—which is also the most accurate star map, for a sphere cannot be projected accurately onto a flat plane. A distortion of the star patterns always arises.

A very simple and effective celestial sphere can be made out of a spherical chemistry flask. Fill the flask with enough blue copper sulphate solution to come halfway up the sphere when the neck is turned downward. The solution should have a small amount of dilute sulphuric acid added to stabilize it. Seal the flask with a rubber stopper and draw a circle (say, colored white) round the middle of the sphere (using a chinagraph pencil designed for glass) tracing the surface edge of the blue liquid when the flask is placed with the neck straight down. Draw a second circle (say, colored red) at an angle of 23-1/2 degrees to the first, its center being also the center of the sphere. Tilt the flask so that its axis through the neck is 52 degrees from horizontal (Figure 31).

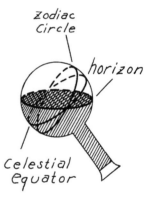

Figure 31

The surface of the liquid now represents the plane of the horizon for an observer at latitude 52 degrees north; the white circle is the celestial equator, and the red circle is the ecliptic, the line through the middle of the zodiac. To rotate the flask round its axis is to reflect exactly the relationship of the zodiac to the horizon and to the celestial equator at any particular time of day or of the year.

Tilting the axis of the flask to any degree from the horizontal gives the sky situation for the same degree of latitude. One can simulate the star movements (rotation of the flask round its axis) for the observer at the geographical poles, at the equator, or anywhere between.

Understanding the relationship of the zodiac to the horizon and to the celestial equator is central to an understanding of observational astronomy, and it is worth spending time on making a celestial sphere or procuring one for demonstration.

The ecliptic, the red line on our globe, is the path of the Sun round the zodiac in a year. We shall leave further discussion of this until later. For now the red line marks the middle of the zodiac and it gives us an indication of how the zodiacal constellations behave.

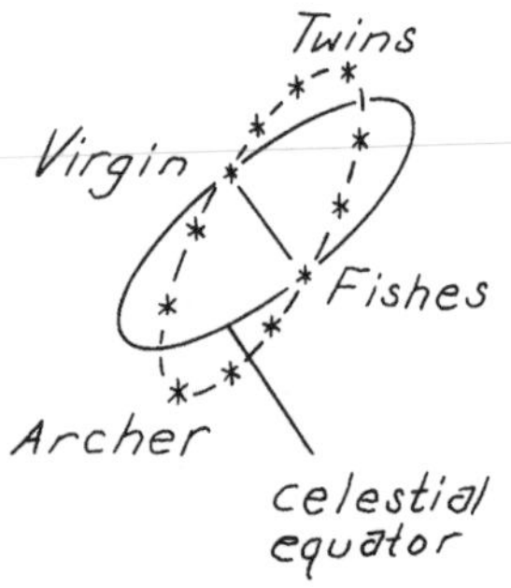

Figure 32

One can picture how some of the zodiacal constellations lie above the celestial equator and some below (Figure 32). The constellations of the Fishes and the Virgin are on the celestial equator, while the Twins is at the highest point above it and the Archer is furthest below.* It must be emphasized that these names, translated from the Latin, relate to the visible star patterns in the sky and not to the "signs" of the zodiac (for example, the ones used by astrologers and designated as "birth signs"). The zodiac of signs and the zodiac of visible stars have shifted in relationship to each other over thousands of years, because of the slow movement of the celestial pole mentioned in Chapter 1. But there is no reason to explain that at this stage, only to emphasize that it is the visible star constellations which are referred to here.

If one now rotates a model celestial globe set for, say, 52 degrees north latitude as shown, then in one complete rotation round the axis the zodiac can be seen to weave round the sky, sometimes standing high above the horizon, or low above it; sometimes cutting the horizon at the east/west points, or northeast/southwest, or southeast/northwest. It will do all

---

* These positions are correct if the zodiacal constellations are considered equal in arc length, with the star Aldebaran in the middle of the constellation of the Bull (see the author's *Astronomy and the Imagination*, p.43). But if the conventional, unequal division of the zodiac laid down by the International Astronomical Union is adhered to, then the highest point of the zodiac (summer solstice) moved from the Twins into the Bull in December, 1989—because of the precession of the equinoxes. The other seasonal points, however, will remain in the present constellations named in Figure 32, for the next few hundred years.

this in one day. It will also be noticed that the celestial equator keeps to a fixed angle above the horizon and cuts it exactly east and west at all times. This must be so, since the plane of the celestial equator is at right angles to the polar axis (Figure 33).

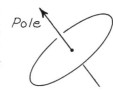

Figure 33

For the present purpose of describing the zodiac, we shall stop the celestial sphere in its rotation in two opposite positions (Figures 34 and 35) and draw maps for each. A further examination of the zodiacal movements in the course of the day and the year is left to the next chapter. The two positions are, firstly, as in Figure 31, and secondly, with the sphere rotated through 180 degrees.

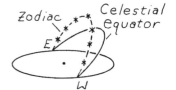

Figure 34

In the first case the zodiac curves furthest above the celestial equator, and in the second case it curves furthest below it, with both arcs cutting the horizon at east and west. The part of the sky to be mapped in both cases is shown in Figure 36. The broad band of the sphere depicted can be flattened (although with some distortion) onto a plane. This is a suitable way to draw the zodiac and its nearby stars. As opposed to the "equatorial" system used for the northern stars, this method is the "horizontal" system, because it is related to the horizon—i.e., measurements in degrees are made along the horizon (azimuth) and perpendicularly above it (altitude). This gives rise to a grid which is shown below in Figure 37—0 degrees being chosen here for the south point for simplicity, with numbers increasing left and right. (This is not the professional method of numbering —see "azimuth" in Appendix 7.)

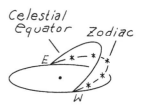

Figure 35

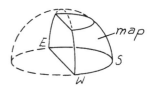

Figure 36

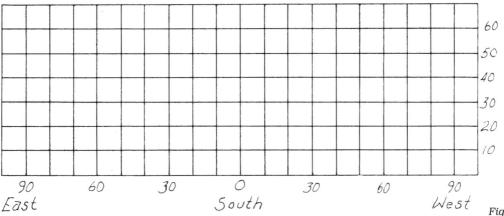

Figure 37

Castor and Pollux, the two main stars of the TWINS (Gemini) have long been regarded by different peoples as twins. A Euphratean star list describes them as the Heaven and Earth Pair. The names come from two Greek heroes—the immortal Pollux, son of Zeus, and Castor, the mortal son of an earthly father. Castor was killed in battle and, at the request of Pollux, they remained together by spending their time alternating between the upper and lower worlds. The Twins, as guardians of Rome, were inscribed on Roman silver coins. They often formed figureheads on the prows of Roman ships and were symbolized by the figure of two stars over a ship. When both stars appeared in the sky, they were considered harbingers of fair weather, and when both could not be seen it meant storms. Castor and Pollux were both sons of Queen Leda, and Greek sailors called them the Ledean Lights. Pollux is the brighter star of the two.

The forecast of weather conditions was also attached to the faint constellation of the CRAB (Cancer) in early times. It possesses a dim, misty patch (a cluster of tiny stars) named Praesepe, from the Latin meaning a stable, manger, or hive. In English astronomical folklore it is known as the Beehive. Violent storms were expected if the misty patch was not visible in a clear sky. The constellation of the Crab has been variously associated with creatures with hard shells, such as the tortoise and beetle (Egypt). In Greek legend it was the crab which seized the foot of Hercules when, in his second labor, he fought a nine-headed monster, an offspring of Typhon. According to the Chaldeans and the Greeks, in that part of the sky occupied by the Crab lay the Gate of Men through which souls descended into human bodies.

In Greek legend, the constellation of the LION (Leo) represented the lion which Hercules slew in his first labor. The ancient Persians had an emblem of the Sun in the constellation of the Lion on their national banner. The ancient Greeks called its chief star "the little king," which is the meaning of the name "Regulus" given to it in Renaissance Europe. Sovereignty has often been attached to this star—cuneiform scripts from the Euphratean valley referred to it as the Star of the King; in India it was the Mighty; in Persia the Center; among the Turanians the Hero; and the Romans called it the Royal Star.

The image of a female deity has long been associated with the constellation of the VIRGIN (Virgo) by early cultures. The Romans saw it as Proserpina (Persephone), who was carried off into the underworld by Pluto to be his wife, but was later allowed to return to the ordinary world for two-thirds of the year. Ancient star maps often depict the Virgin as a winged woman holding stalks of wheat or corn in her left hand. In Egypt the constellation was connected with the goddess Isis, who formed the Milky Way by dropping wheat across the sky. In India the constellation was known as the Maiden and in the valley of the Euphrates it was associated with the goddess Ishtar, daughter of heaven and queen of the stars. In Peru the constellation was the Magic Mother or Earth Mother, and in Assyria it was the Wife of Bel (Marduk). The name of its principal star, Spica, comes from the Latin meaning Ear of Grain. The star lies where the maiden is usually shown holding stalks of corn. The Arabs called Spica the Defenseless or Unarmed One, as well as the Solitary One, because it lacks bright companions.

The concept of a weighing balance for the constellation of the SCALES (Libra) seems to have come originally from Egypt. Libra is the only zodiacal constellation not represented today by an animal or human being. At one stage the scales were shown being held by the figure of a man, and the Romans represented him as Julius Caesar. The Greeks, however, did not recognize this area of the sky as a separate constellation and showed it as the claws of the neighboring Scorpion. The Hebrews saw it as a scale-beam, while the Chinese occupied this area with a dragon, their national emblem.

Greek mythology assigns the constellation of the SCORPION (Scorpius) to that creature which sprang out of the earth and stung to death the giant hunter Orion. The Akkadians called the constellation the Seizer or Stinger, and the Place Where One Bows Down. The Mayans of Mexico referred to it as the Sign of the Death God. Some authorities claim that at the time of Abraham this constellation was called the Eagle, and in the civilizations of the Euphrates its chief star, Antares, was sometimes known as the Day-Heaven Bird. The name Antares comes from the Greek meaning similar to, or in place of, Mars; and the star has a reddish color. The Chinese knew it as the Fire Star.

The constellation of the ARCHER (Sagittarius) is depicted on old Babylonian monuments and in early zodiacs of Egypt and India. In India its name simply means Arrow. The Greek astronomer Eratosthenes described it as a Satyr, and it was also depicted as the wise centaur Chiron with his bow and arrow, he being renowned for his skill in hunting, medicine, music, gymnastics, and prophecy. He was struck accidentally by a poisoned arrow and was placed among the stars by Zeus. Cuneiform texts describe the Archer as the Strong One, the Giant of War, and the Illuminator of the Great City.

The constellation of the GOAT (Capricornus) is in that region of the sky described anciently as the Sea, and has been known as the Sea Goat or goat with a fish's tail. It was, in addition, called the Double Ship. The Greeks also named it after their god Pan. In the ancient East the constellation was known as the Southern Gate of the Sun. The Greeks also described it as the Gate of the Gods, through which the souls of the dead passed into the other world—as opposed to the Gate of Men, through which souls descended to Earth in the opposite constellation of the Crab.

True to its name, the constellation of the WATERMAN (Aquarius) along with the neighboring Sea Goat and Fishes, is placed in that part of the sky anciently pictured as a celestial sea. Below this constellation is another which is called the Southern Fish (Piscis Austrinus) and includes the star Fomalhaut, from the Arabic meaning fish's mouth. Early images of the Waterman show a man or boy pouring water from a jar into the Southern Fish's mouth. In India the Waterman constellation was called Water Jar and in Peru it was the Mother of Waters. In Greece it was the beautiful youth Ganymede, cup-bearer to Zeus and responsible for the annual flooding of the river Nile.

In early legends the Southern Fish was the parent of the two fishes which constitute the zodiacal constellation of the FISHES (Pisces). The Greeks identified the two fish with Venus and Cupid, who took on this form when they leaped into the river Euphrates to escape the giant Typhon. The Babylonians, Syrians, Persians, and Turks also depicted this constellation as comprising two fish. They also figured in the Hebrew zodiac and the Fishes was considered the national constellation of the Jews, a tradition being that a special conjunction of the planets Jupiter and Saturn took place in it three years before the birth of Moses. There was another such conjunction in the Fishes in 7 B.C., sometimes considered today to be connected with, or a herald of, the birth of Christ.

These, then, are brief descriptions of some of the mythologies associated with the stars of the zodiac. I leave the above account as an example of the richness of the subject and as a stimulation to further research on the part of the teacher or student in the pursuit of humanizing the heavens again and bringing the subject of astronomy alive in the imagination as well as clear in the thinking.

Supplementary Exercises

An alternative to drawing the zodiac by the grid method in Figures 38 and 39 is to draw the constellations freehand as they stretch between east and west. For this it would be useful to know the curve of the celestial equator above the horizon. Once the celestial equator has been established in altitude and azimuth for a particular latitude, the zodiac can be drawn above or below it in its positions for midwinter midnight or midsummer midnight. The celestial equator, thus drawn, is not a semicircle or an ellipse, but an oval on the plane of the page. It is also the path of a star rising due east, and other star "trails" can be made parallel to it to give a representation of star movement (see Figure 8).

For a geographical latitude of 52 degrees north, the curve of the celestial equator is as shown in Figure 40, with the star Procyon following it closely. Here seven points on the curve have been found before drawing it freehand.

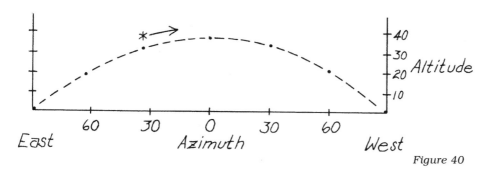

Figure 40

The highest point is the colatitude (90 degrees minus 52 degrees = 38 degrees) of the location at 52 degrees on Earth. To find other points above the horizon one can use a celestial globe set to one's latitude. A strip of paper graduated 90—0 (the same as the measurements for declination on the globe) is laid from the topmost point of the globe (overhead position, not the pole) down to the horizon, with the 90 degree mark at overhead. With this one can measure the altitude of the celestial equator above the horizon in, say, southeast and southwest directions. For example, at a latitude of 30 degrees the celestial equator is found to be at an altitude of about 51 degrees above the southeast and southwest points on the horizon (45 degrees east and west of south). Approximate values for the altitude of the celestial equator in SE and SW directions at some other latitudes are: latitude 40—altitude 40; latitude 50—altitude 31; latitude 60—altitude 22.

The zodiacal constellations can now be drawn freehand above or below the celestial equator, as in Figures 38 and 39. If desired, correct due south positions for the line (the ecliptic) through the center of the zodiac can be found by placing a point either 23-1/2 degrees above or below the topmost point of the celestial equator.

A simpler method is to mark the due south position of the celestial equator (observer's colatitude) above the horizon, mark the due south position of the ecliptic above or below it (for midwinter midnight or midsummer midnight) and draw freehand the curves of the celestial equator and ecliptic through these points from east to west.

Star trails with respect to a northern straight-line horizon (Figure 6) can be found by plotting the altitude and azimuth of stars as they move, using the same method of measurement on the celestial globe as above.

Chapter Three

The Sun

As everyone knows, the Sun rises in the east and sets in the west. If this were all it did, life on this Earth would be very different from how we know it. As it happens, the Sun also rises sometimes toward the northeast and sometimes southeast, and this seemingly simple addition brings about a whole rhythm of seasons within which nature, climate, and civilization have evolved. The Sun's different rising points have brought movement into the life of nature and human beings.

The basic phenomenon concerning the Sun's positions on the horizon is that, when rising over the course of a year, its positions move left and right, as in Figure 41.

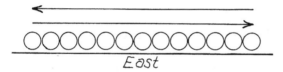

Figure 41

It rises from each of these positions at an angle which is the observer's latitude subtracted from 90. So at a latitude of 50 degrees north, it will rise to the right at an angle (as represented on a flat plane) of 40 degrees. Its horizon position at midsummer will be north of east, in the autumn due east, at midwinter south of east, and in the spring due east again (Figure 42).

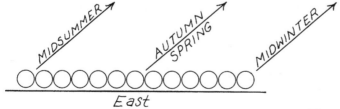

Figure 42

This movement is reflected in the west at sunset, as in Figure 43, where the Sun sets at the same angle in which it rose.

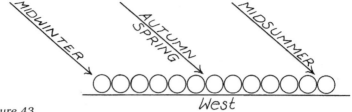

Figure 43

Taking the southern horizon and completing the picture, the Sun in the four seasons can be represented as in Figure 44, following the shape of the oval curve of the celestial equator described in Figure 40 of the last chapter.

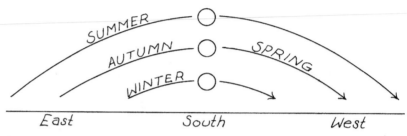

Figure 44

It can now be seen that looking toward the south during the course of one year, the Sun makes an arc sometimes higher, sometimes lower than the celestial equator which curves from due east to due west and along which the Sun travels on the autumn and spring equinoxes. Winter, for example, is accompanied by a low, small arc, which shortens daylight and brings less warmth.

An explanation as to why the Sun makes such movements can be found on the celestial globe in Figure 31. Because the Sun in one year moves round its path (the ecliptic) once, passing through the zodiacal stars, it is sometimes above the celestial equator, sometimes below it, and twice lies on it.

When the Sun is in the constellation of the Twins it is summer in the Northern Hemisphere,* and when the sun is in the constellation of the Archer it is winter. In connection with this,

* See footnote page 14.

one can consider the subsequent paths above the horizon of the different zodiacal constellations. Each constellation always follows its same path in rising and setting, whatever the time of year. When the Sun enters a constellation, it shares the regular daily journey of those stars. It is summer in the Northern Hemisphere when the Sun is in the Twins because this constellation makes the highest and widest arc of all the zodiacal constellations, the others making curves at various distances below it. The situation is, in general, as shown in Figure 45.

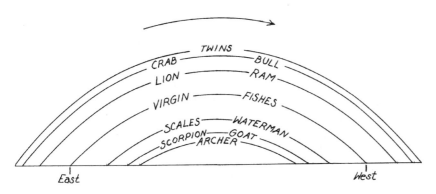

Figure 45

The seasons can be expressed in various ways, and another way for Earth-centered observation is to experience the Sun spiralling round the Earth from day to day (Figure 46).

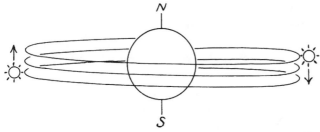

Figure 46

Here the Sun is, of course, much further away than shown, but the effect is to create in six months a season when the north pole is in continuous daylight and the south pole in continuous darkness; a season when day and night are equal all over the Earth; and a season when the south pole is in continuous daylight and the north pole in continuous darkness (Figures 47, 48, 49).

Figure 47

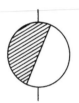

Figure 48

Figure 49

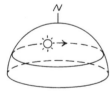

Figure 52

Figure 53

A further way of demonstrating the seasons as experienced from Earth is to show the ecliptic lying at an angle to the equator, and the Sun's position on it during the year determining the area of darkness (Figure 50). In this case, the Earth must be seen to rotate on its axis in one day.

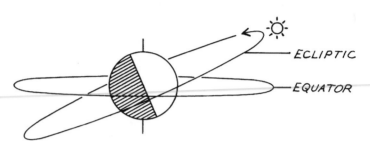

ECLIPTIC

EQUATOR

Figure 50

A further step is to picture the rotating and constantly-tilted Earth orbiting round the Sun (Figure 51), which is common in textbooks. In this chapter the Earth observer's direct experience is taken into account first.

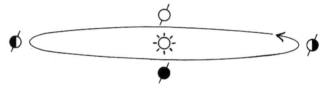

Figure 51

Mention of the Earth's poles raises the question of how the Sun is experienced at extreme latitudes. One's latitude determines a particular geography and, along with it, a particular relationship to the sky. In summer at the north pole the Sun spirals up and down the sky in six months, making a near-circle in one day. Daily, in relation to the horizon, it moves horizontally from left to right (Figures 52 and 53). The Moon, planets, and stars make the same sort of daily horizontal motion. In fact the stars above the horizon continuously circle (not spiral) and never set, whereas the stars below the horizon never rise. The celestial equator lies along the horizon. Day and night at the poles lasts one year. Dawn lasts almost two months; the Sun appears above the horizon for about six months; dusk is almost two months; and there is dark night for about two and one-half months. At the south pole the Sun, Moon, planets, and stars move above the horizon in a right-to-left horizontal direction.

An opposite situation to the poles takes place at the Earth's equator. There, day and night last roughly twelve hours each throughout the year, the Sun always rising at about 6 a.m. and setting at about 6 p.m. (Figure 54). The poles lie on the horizon, and the celestial equator rules the skies, one expression of this being that at midsummer at the equator (when the Sun passes overhead) the Sun then lies on the celestial equator, at one of the equinox points. So there are two technical midsummers a year. Another consequence of the poles lying on the horizon is that as the sky turns, all constellations on the celestial sphere rise and set, and are therefore at some time visible. At the poles only half of the sphere of stars is visible, the other half never being seen.

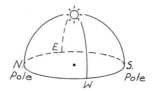

Figure 54

Part way between the poles and the equator are borderline regions for day and night. These regions lie near the Arctic and Antarctic Circles, which are 66-1/2 degrees north and south. Further toward the poles from these regions, periods of darkness or periods of daylight can exceed 24 hours each, while further toward the equator, all nights or periods of daylight are less than 24 hours each. The Arctic and Antarctic latitudes (66 degrees 34 minutes) are the demarcation areas because, seen from them, the celestial equator is at an angle of 23 degrees 26 minutes to the horizon; that is, the celestial equator, at its highest point, is this amount above the horizon. This angle is also the angle between the celestial equator and the ecliptic. So when the Sun is at its highest point above the celestial equator at midsummer noon, it climbs this angle x 2 = 46 degrees 52 minutes above the horizon. On the other side of the sky, the celestial equator is 23 degrees 26 minutes below the horizon, so at midnight the Sun is the same distance above this, which is on the horizon itself. This means that at midsummer the Sun does not set, but just skims the horizon (Figure 55). To find this situation readily on a celestial globe, first turn the sphere so that the ecliptic coincides with the horizon.

Figure 55

Other borderline zones are the regions on Earth beyond which the Sun cannot stand overhead at midday. These are the Tropic of Cancer in the Northern Hemisphere and the Tropic of Capricorn in the Southern. Both are 23-1/2 degrees from the equator. For example, at midsummer in the Northern Hemisphere the Sun cannot stand overhead much further north than Havana in Cuba, and at midsummer in the Southern Hemisphere it cannot stand overhead further south than about São Paulo in Brazil. It should be noted that, whatever rhythm the seasons bring, all places on Earth receive the same amount of daylight in one year.

The seasons are also expressed in the lengths and directions of the Sun's shadow during the year. At noon in summer the shadow of a stick is shorter than it is at noon in winter. At each season the tip of the shadow traces out a line on the ground which is curved—apart from the two dates of the spring and autumn equinoxes, when it is a straight line. The reason for the straight line is that when the Sun rises due east and sets due west, the plane of its movement passes through the top of the stick. The observer also stands within this plane. Since the Sun is so far away, the height of the stick is of no consequence (Figure 56). The curves for summer and winter are hyperbolas, mirroring the Sun's rising and setting toward the north in summer, and south in winter (Figure 57).

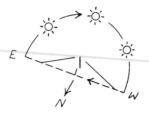

Figure 56

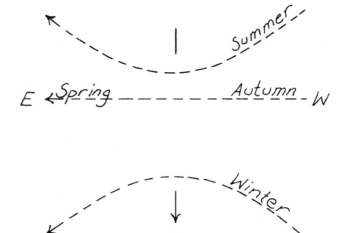

Figure 57

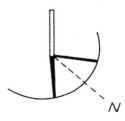

Figure 58

The determination of local noon and true north and south directions can be found using a vertical stick on a horizontal surface. Because the movement of the shadow tip is symmetrical on either side (east and west) of the stick, a circle drawn with the foot of the stick as center will be touched by the line of the shadow tip at equal times on either side of noon. If these touching points are marked and the angle they make with the base of the stick halved, this will give a line running due north and south, along which the shadow will lie at local noon (Figure 58).

This device is called a noon mark and was commonly used in earlier times. It gives local apparent noon, which is the true Sun's noon for a particular place, midway between sunrise and sunset. This is distinct from local mean time, and also from standard mean time in a particular zone to which we set our clocks (discounting Summer Time or Daylight Saving Time).

An early and very successful attempt at measuring the circumference of the Earth used the Sun's shadow. The calculation was done by the scholar Eratosthenes of Alexandria around 200 B.C. He understood that Alexandria and the town of Syene (now called Aswan) were on the same line of longitude and that at noon on Midsummer Day the Sun stood exactly overhead at Syene. This meant that a gnomon (which casts the shadow on a sundial), if perpendicular, would in fact, cast no shadow at that moment. He then measured the angle at which a shadow *was* cast by a perpendicular gnomon (in the middle of a bowl-shaped sundial) at noon on the same day at Alexandria. He measured this angle as 1/50th of a circle—that is, the angle at the top of the gnomon standing at A in Figure 59, where A represents Alexandria and S represents Syene. The drawing is schematic only, in order to show the principle. The directions to the Sun from the two places can be considered as parallel since the Sun is so far away.

The angle of the Sun's shadow to the gnomon at A is the same as the angle at the center of the Earth at O. So the angle at O is proportional to the arc AS. Eratosthenes found the angle at O to be 1/50th of a circle, so AS was 1/50th of the Earth's circumference. A modern school atlas (using conical projection) shows the two places to be separated by about 1/48th of the Earth's polar circumference (calculated on a sphere, as with Eratosthenes). It turns out that Eratosthenes was incorrect in assuming that the midsummer Sun stood exactly overhead at Syene or that the two places were due north and south of each other. Even so, it was a brilliant method and came close to the correct answer.

Whether one imagines the Earth to be rotating on its axis in 24 hours or the Sun to circle the sky in that time, the result is that, at any one moment, all times of day and night stretch round the Earth and are in movement round it. There is a

PLATE 3
A medieval noon mark in *La Gnomonique pratique*, by Bedos de Celles; Paris, 1790.

From *Sundials: Their Theory and Construction*, by Albert Waugh; Dover, New York, 1973.

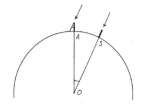

Figure 59

sunrise accompanied by the dawn chorus of birds, perpetually circling the earth. Likewise, sunset, midnight, and noon make their circuits in 24 hours. Any particular city, for instance, has these times of day or night sweep over it. But if we travel east or west we shorten or lengthen the day by moving toward the approaching Sun which comes from the east, or by moving with it as we go west. To travel even a few miles alters the length of the actual day. To go from London to Paris shortens the actual day by more than 8 minutes.

To keep on travelling east and return to one's starting place means to experience one whole day more than someone who remains at the starting place. To travel west round the world subtracts a day in terms of one's experience of, say, sunrises. Perhaps this can best be seen by imagining that one travels west at the same speed as the daily Sun in the sky. If it is noon when beginning one's journey, then it will remain noon for 24 hours until one returns to the starting point. But someone who stays at the starting place will experience noon, sunset, midnight, sunrise, and noon again. Travelling east round the world makes the Sun appear to rise and set faster than normal. If one starts out eastward at noon and travels as fast as the Sun to half-way round the world, the Sun will have travelled half-way in the opposite direction and it will be noon again. Another half circuit brings noon yet again where one started from—an experience of two days during one circuit of the Sun.

Therefore, in travelling east round the world, one must subtract a day at some point to keep the date the same as that kept by those at the place of origin. In travelling west round the world, a day must be added at some point. A mistake was made through neglecting this fact by the very first voyagers round the world. The ships of the Portuguese navigator Ferdinand Magellan sailed westward from Spain in 1519, and the surviving ship reached the Cape Verde Islands in 1522. The captain calculated that the day of his arrival was Wednesday, July 19, but was astonished to learn that it was, in fact Thursday, July 20.

In order to standardize the situation, it has to be determined *where* a traveller adds or subtracts a day. This place can also determine where a particular date is first experienced, for the start of a day must be born somewhere before it circles round the Earth. The day conventionally begins at midnight. So there has to be a line which, when midnight lies along it, the same day is kept all over the Earth (say Wednesday). Looking down on the north pole of the Earth, this line is the broken one in Figure 60.

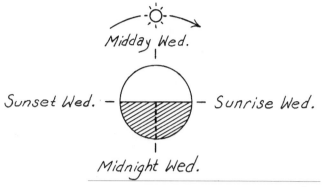

Figure 60

But as the Sun moves clockwise, the midnight point moves also. Places on the broken line now experience a time after midnight, in the early hours of the next day (Figure 61).

Figure 61

The area between midnight and 3 a.m. has moved into Thursday. As the midday Sun proceeds further, that part of the Earth experiencing Wednesday becomes smaller while the part of the Earth experiencing Thursday becomes larger (Figure 62).

So midnight, with its change of date, now sweeps around the Earth, but the broken line is left with different days on either side of it too. This continues until the midnight line coincides again with the broken line, and it is Thursday everywhere.

Figure 62

The broken line in Figure 60 lies on the Date Line and on Earth is marked out by the 180th meridian, as was internationally agreed in 1845. It is the line from pole to pole on the opposite side of the Earth from Greenwich, London. The Date Line only deviates from this line of longitude to avoid dividing certain land areas into permanently separate dates. But on crossing the line by sea or air, one must move forward a day travelling westward with the Sun (clockwise in Figure 60) and move back a day travelling eastward. Magellan's captain followed the Sun, and after having circumnavigated the world his Wednesday should have become Thursday.

To find their position at sea, Magellan's sailors used their knowledge of astronomy. With the instruments at their disposal for measuring the positions of Sun or stars, it was comparatively easy to find their latitude, but finding *longitude* was a difficult problem.

As shown in Figure 54, at the geographical equator the celestial equator passes overhead. To travel north by a certain number of degrees means that the north pole of the sky will rise by the same amount above the horizon, until at the north pole itself it will stand overhead. Therefore, measuring the height (altitude) of the pole above the horizon, being helped in the Northern Hemisphere by the presence of Polaris and other stars, directly gives one's latitude in degrees. This is one way of approaching it. Also, knowing what the celestial positions of the Sun or a star were from tables, seamen then measured their altitudes above the horizon.

The problem in finding *longitude* is connected with our previous considerations of how time alters as one travels east or west. In a sense, you take your day with you and experience, say, noon at a moment different from anyone at a different longitude. The requirement is to find one's distance east or west from the starting point. One cannot easily or accurately know this unless one knows the time held by those at the starting point. If one does know it, the difference between this and one's own time will give the longitude—15 degrees for every hour. One way of knowing the time kept by the place of origin is to carry a watch which keeps that time, but it must be very accurate. For example, an error of four seconds in time is equivalent to one nautical mile (east or west) at the equator.

In Magellan's day, no such timekeeper had been invented. It was a common practice to sail to the latitude of the place of destination, then sail to the place along that line of latitude—a costly operation in terms of time and provisions, and not even always possible because of the lie of the land.

During the lifetime of the explorer Captain James Cook, a watch which kept very accurate time despite the rigors of sea voyage was invented and made by the Yorkshireman John Harrison. The watch, a large silver one, was called a chronometer, and a replica of the instrument was taken on Captain Cook's second voyage to the South Seas from 1772–1775. It kept such precise time that Captain Cook referred to it in his journal as "our trusty friend, the Watch," or "our never-failing guide."

PLATE 4
Meridian altitude observation of the sun by sea astrolabe in *Regimiento de Navegacion* (1563) by Pedro de Medina.

From *Science and the Techniques of Navigation in the Renaissance* (National Maritime Museum, Maritime Monographs and Reports No. 19, 1974, Greenwich, London).

Before the voyage, the chronometer would have been set to keep Plymouth time, the port of departure. To make it simpler for our present purpose, let us imagine that it is set to Greenwich (London) time, Greenwich being on the zero degree line of longitude. The days on which Captain Cook sailed eastward (travelling against the daily motion of the Sun) were shorter than the full days marked out by the chronometer, so the time shown on the chronometer fell behind in comparison to, say, local noons on the journey.

The voyage took them south of the equator so that the south celestial pole was now the point above the horizon round which the stars turned. After about eight months, and not long before land was sighted on March 25, 1773, we can imagine the navigator calculating, by the stars, the height of the south celestial pole above the horizon—and finding it to be 46 degrees. Therefore, they are at latitude 46 degrees south. This would be checked by observing the height of the Sun above the horizon (perhaps at local noon) and consulting tables showing the Sun's current position (latitude) on the celestial sphere. Also, at that moment of local noon, determined with a sundial, the chronometer is found to be 11 hours 4 minutes slow on local time. Where is the ship?

The information they have is that they are 46 degrees south of the equator and 11 hours 4 minutes east of Greenwich. The answer is found by converting time into degrees of longitude. Four minutes of time are equivalent to 1 degree of longitude.

Converting 11 hours 4 minutes into minutes gives 664 minutes. Dividing by four (1 degree) gives 166 degrees east of Greenwich.

Soon afterward they sight the southern tip of New Zealand. They anchor in Dusky Bay and later sail on to an island which is named Resolution Island, after their ship, HMS *Resolution.*

The above is only an approximation of the geographical position and the method of determining it, to allow simple calculation, but it is sufficient to show a process. Other examples can be chosen for classroom practice.

Such, then, are the basic movements of the Sun and stars seen from Earth and their importance for human life on land and sea. Without a knowledge of the heavens human beings are lost on Earth. Time and space elude their grasp.

Supplementary Exercises

1.

The construction of a sundial is a useful activity following on from the noon mark determination in Figure 58. The simplest form is an equatorial sundial which does not require complicated geometry and, once made, can be adjusted to any geographical latitude. Draw a square on a piece of cardboard and mark its center point. Use this point as the center of a circle drawn inside the square. Divide the circle into 24 equal parts. Number the divisions as in figure 63. Draw a circle of the same size with the same center point, on the other side of the square. Divide it also into 24 and number as in figure 64. Cut out the square and make a hole in the center into which you can fit a cylindrical stick at right angles to the plane of the square. Place the square on edge on a level surface with the number 12 at the bottom, resting the end of the stick on the flat surface. The dial marked "Front" should now be uppermost and the stick aligned south-north. Adjust the stick by sliding it through the hole so that when the sundial is placed on the flat surface, the stick points upward at the north celestial pole—that is, the angle ABC in figure 65 is the same as your latitude. Alternatively, the angle BCD should be your colatitude, that is, 90 degrees minus your latitude. If ABC is 40 degrees, then BCD will be 50 degrees.

FRONT

Figure 63

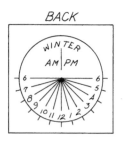

BACK

Figure 64

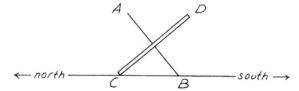

Figure 65

The plane of the square (indicated by the line CD) will be in the plane of the celestial equator. When the Sun is above the celestial equator in summer, the stick's shadow on the top face of the dial will show local apparent time. When the Sun is below the celestial equator in winter, the shadow on the bottom face will show the time.

This model can be made more rigidly in wood, metal, etc., so that the stick firmly keeps a 90-degree angle with the plane of the dial. The dial can be made to hinge to a base and different latitudes can be measured, and marks for the positions of the stick made on the base. Then it becomes a travelling dial, popular before clocks and watches became common. Some dials have a magnetic compass attached to them to find north, though it must be noted that magnetic north is not necessarily true north, and a correction is usually required if one wishes accuracy.

The dial will not show the same time as kept by clocks. For it to do so, two corrections are necessary. Firstly, the clock keeps "mean" time, reflecting an average movement for the Sun. The sundial faithfully follows the Sun's actual motion, which is irregular, and this needs to be evened out. In winter the Sun moves faster through the constellations than in summer. Since the Earth rotates in the same direction in which the Sun appears to move through the constellations, this lengthens the day slightly during winter. In addition, the Sun moves (along the ecliptic) at an angle to the sky's daily motion—the daily motion being parallel to the celestial equator. The end result is that, in the course of a year, there are two periods when a sundial is behind local mean time, two periods when it is ahead, and four times when it coincides with local mean time. This discrepancy is expressed by what is called the equation of time. Figure 66 gives a graphic picture of the situation, and such diagrams are sometimes etched on sundials.

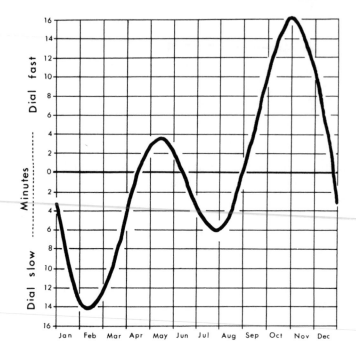

Figure 66

From *Sundials: Their Theory and Construction,* by Albert Waugh; Dover, New York, 1973.

Secondly, the clock will be set to a "standard" mean time relating to a particular area. For example, in Britain all clocks keep the same mean time as that experienced along the 0-degree line of longitude which passes through London. In the United States, residents of Boston or Detroit keep Eastern Standard Time which is true to the longitude line 75 degrees west of London (Greenwich). So, if you use the sundial at a place west of your standard meridian (line of longitude), time must be added to adjust to that meridian at a rate of 4 minutes for every degree. (Sundial time east of one's standard meridian requires the difference of longitude to be subtracted at the same rate of 4 minutes per degree.) For example, a sundial 3 degrees west of its standard meridian on September 25 must have 12 minutes added to what it reads to account for longitude, and 8 minutes subtracted to account for mean time (using the equation of time), which means that the sundial was 4 minutes slower than a clock on that day. The accuracy or positioning of a sundial can be checked by doing the procedure in reverse.

It should not be forgotten that during the summer, standard time is likely to be advanced an hour by "Summer Time" or "Daylight Saving Time".

2.

Finding the height (altitude) of a celestial object can be achieved with a simple instrument called a clinometer. If used to measure the height of the Pole Star, this gives one's approximate latitude on Earth. The instrument can easily be made from a geometrical protractor; a large blackboard protractor is useful for demonstration. Attach a plumb line to the center point of the semicircle (Figure 67). Holding the protractor with its plane vertical, aim the straight edge at the star, and the plumb line will show the altitude in the number of degrees it hangs away from the middle of the semi-circumference. This can be done in conditions of twilight when the star first appears. Sights or a sighting tube can be fixed on the straight edge for greater accuracy, and the instrument can be screwed to a stand. Set up in this way, it can measure the altitude of the Sun when the light is seen to pass through the tube onto a piece of card. But the Sun must never be looked at with a clinometer because the brightness of the Sun will cause eye damage.

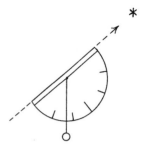

Figure 67

Another elementary way of finding the altitude of the Sun is to measure the length of the shadow of a vertical stick (gnomon), then measure the height of the stick, and use these lengths to draw two sides of a right-angled triangle. The third side, from the tip of the stick to the tip of the shadow, will give an angle to the base line, which is the altitude of the Sun (Figure 68).

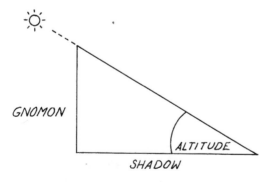

GNOMON

ALTITUDE

SHADOW   *Figure 68*

For better accuracy, a small hole can be made near the top of the stick for the Sun to shine through and make a spot on the ground or a flat, white surface from which measurements can be made. If the measurements are done at local apparent noon, one can work out the position of the Sun in the zodiac, based on the principle of Figure 45. For example, one's colatitude gives the altitude of the celestial equator due south, and the zodiacal constellations are positioned in stages extending 23-1/2 degrees above and below this. A celestial globe or planisphere will show the zodiac's height above or below the equator, or the zodiac's altitude, when these are measured directly above the due south horizon point.

3.

Use of the properties of similar triangles was made by the Greek philosopher Thales (c. 624-547 B.C.) to measure the height of an Egyptian pyramid. He placed a vertical gnomon in the ground and its shadow formed two sides of a triangle, which lengths he then measured. This triangle reproduced the same proportions of the large triangle formed by the height of the pyramid and the end of the pyramid's shadow (Figure 69). For example, let us imagine the Sun due east of the Great Pyramid of Khufu at Giza. If the length of the shadow of the gnomon is twice the gnomon's height, and the distance from the gnomon to the base center of the pyramid is 908 feet, then one knows that the height of the pyramid is half that, 454 feet. It is said that the Egyptian king Amasis II was amazed at this use of an abstract geometrical principle to solve such a problem. (In the calculation, the Sun is so distant from the earth that two shadow edges which it casts are virtually parallel.)

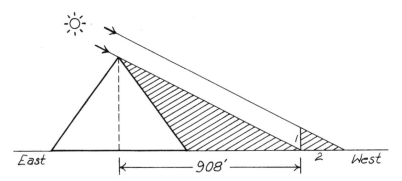

Figure 69

It should be added that many fanciful things have been written about the Great Pyramid, one of them being that when it was built in about 2800 B.C. the entrance tunnel or "descending passage" pointed to the (then) Pole Star called Thuban in the constellation of the Dragon. This is not the case.* The star could be seen up the entrance tunnel many centuries before

*See: *Sky and Telescope*, June 1985, p. 496.

and after, but not during, the period around 2800 B.C. The passage is at an angle of 26.523 degrees to horizontal, and therefore does not point to the north celestial pole either since the pyramid's latitude is about 30 degrees north.

Another suggestion, often occurring in literature, has been that stars can be seen during daytime reflected at the bottoms of deep wells or seen from the bottoms of shafts, and so forth. Scientific support for this, based on optical probability, is virtually nil.** A telescope, however, does reveal bright stars during the day. With a telescope the lenses darken the light of the sky but enhance the light of the star, whereas the patch of daylight seen with the naked eye from the bottom of a shaft remains very bright.

4.
Further examples of the path traced on the ground by the tip of the shadow of a vertical stick can be worked out, following on from Figure 57. It can be asked what paths will be traced on the ground at different latitudes.

At the equator, when the Sun is overhead in spring and autumn, the path will be a straight line passing through the base of the stick; the paths in other seasons will produce hyperbolas (Figure 70).

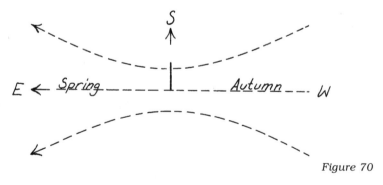

Figure 70

At the Tropics of Cancer and Capricorn which are 23 degrees 26 minutes latitude, the Sun is overhead at noon at midsummer. Therefore the hyperbola of that date will pass through the base of the stick (Figure 71).

**"On seeing Stars (especially up chimneys)," by David Hughes, *Quarterly Journal of the Royal Astronomical Society*, Vol.24, No.3, 1983. Also, "No Tunnel Vision," letter in *Sky & Telescope*, February, 1990.

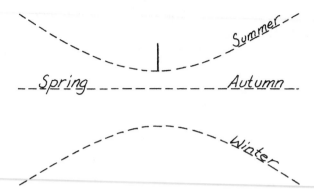

Figure 71

At and beyond the Arctic and Antarctic Circles the shadow tips are able to trace out parabolas. The Arctic and Antarctic Circles are those latitudes where the Sun at midsummer does not set but just skims the horizon. Therefore, at one moment (midnight) the shadow will stretch out to infinity, then shorten again, forming a parabola, a curve which reaches infinity once (a hyperbola reaches it twice)—Figure 72.

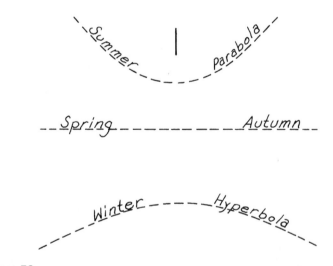

Figure 72

Between the Arctic and Antarctic Circles and the poles, ellipses as well as parabolas and hyperbolas are formed (Figure 73).

At the Earth's poles the midsummer shadow tip will lie on a circle, and the spring and autumn shadows will lengthen to the horizon where another circle will be formed (Figure 74).

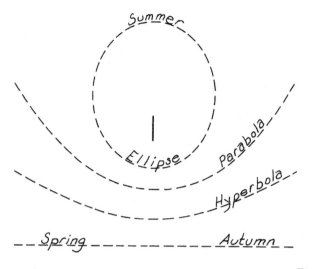

Figure 73

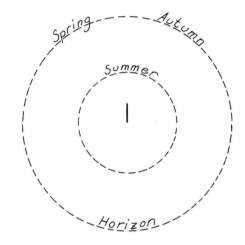

Figure 74

These descriptions are general and assume that the surface on which the curves and lines are traced out is flat and horizontal; they also do not take adjustments due to the Sun's refraction in the atmosphere close to the horizon, etc., into account. But study of such shadow phenomena provides a useful exercise in picturing how the conic curves belong to the same geometrical family and can evolve out of each other by transformation.*

---

*For the preceeding series of diagrams, credit is due to the excellent work in this field of Dr. Hermann von Baravalle, a teacher at the original Waldorf School in Stuttgart and later Chairman of the Mathematics Department of Adelphi College (now University), New York.

Chapter Four

The Moon

The Moon is ruler of the night sky—when it is present and prominent there. The changing from being present to being absent, from appearing bright to dim, is its principle feature for the observer waiting for darkness to fall and the night sky to reveal itself. The reason for the Moon's changeability is that it is not independent as far as light is concerned, but leans on the Sun for illumination. The Moon has been called in early times the Queen of Heaven, but any study of its shapes and movements must include the Sun from which it derives its light.

The first phenomena to be considered then, are its phases which alter from night to night. In one part of the month, the lit area of the Moon grows larger or waxes; in another it grows smaller or wanes until it disappears altogether, only to be reborn a few days later. The basic picture of this is shown in the following two figures.

Figure 75

In Figure 75 the Sun is placed below the western horizon after sunset, and when the sky darkens, the Moon becomes readily visible. The Moon in one month moves from west to east, so the first phase shown is the crescent above the Sun, and the last the full Moon opposite the Sun. The figure represents the Moon's appearance at sunset over a period of two weeks, half of its monthly motion.

To show the other half of this motion above the horizon, we place the Sun in the east at sunrise—at the end of the night which began with the full Moon rising in Figure 75. Again the phases progress from right to left; the full Moon is still opposite the Sun where we left off, but it is now setting (Figure 76). The last phase shown is the crescent. After that, the Sun and Moon are too close together for the Moon to be seen separately (it is hidden in the Sun's light), but when it later emerges on the other side of the Sun, another cycle begins.

Figure 76

Figure 75 shows the Moon waxing during evenings, and Figure 76 shows it waning during mornings. It should be noted that the lit edge nearest the Sun is always directed along the path of a curve (approximately the ecliptic).

This is the picture from day to day in the course of a month. But during each day the whole sky, with Moon and Sun, turns from left to right, or east to west. This means that one particular phase, say half-Moon, makes a daily movement as in Figure 77.

Figure 77

This applies to all the other phases, so when the evening crescent Moon is first seen at sunset, it is in the act of setting and is only briefly visible. The full Moon, on the other hand, is visible all night and rules the heavens.

The evening half-Moon is called first quarter, since the Moon has completed the first quarter of its monthly cycle. Seen from above the Earth, the Moon's movement and shadow would appear as in Figure 78 (inner ring). The phases in Figure 78 are to be experienced from the earth at the center and looking toward the moon. For the lower three phases from waning gibbous to waning crescent, the page should be rotated 180° so that they represent how they appear above the horizon.

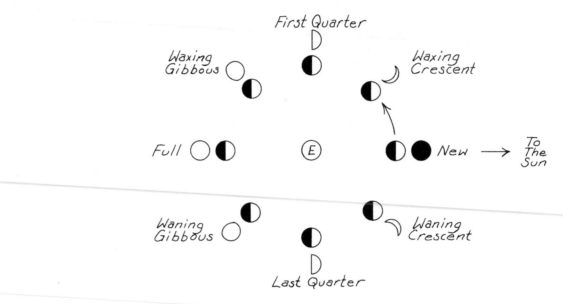

Figure 78

The word "month" is derived from an Old English word for moon, so we are effectively saying "moonth." It takes the Moon 29-1/2 days to pass from new, through its phases, and back to the invisible new Moon again. In early times the calendar month kept to these phases, so that when a full Moon appeared in the evening sky, everyone knew that the month was halfway through. The beginning of the month was announced when the waxing crescent first appeared, or was calculated to appear, in the sky. This not only started the month but also the first day of the month, so that the day began at sunset and ended at the next sunset. Today's generally used calendar no longer follows the movement of the Moon, but that of the Sun (dividing 365-1/4 days into 12 months), though some religions still use the old system.

It should be noted that when the waxing crescent appears in the sky, its tilt to the horizon differs from month to month and, in fact, expresses the seasons. This is because the Moon in its orbit round the Earth fairly closely follows the ecliptic (differing at most by about 5 degrees above or below), and the ecliptic varies its angle to the horizon according to the season. This is best shown on a celestial globe or planisphere. The result is that at sunset during the four seasons of the year the ecliptic assumes different angles to the horizon, as shown in Figures 79, 80, 81, and 82.

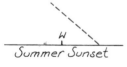

Spring Sunset

Figure 79

Summer Sunset

Figure 80

Autumn Sunset

Figure 81

Winter Sunset

Figure 82

The differing positions of the Sun along the horizon were explained in the last chapter. It will be seen that the angle of the ecliptic to the horizon at sunset is the same in summer and winter, while in spring the angle is steeper and in the autumn flatter. Because the waxing crescent moon lies near the ecliptic, its tilt to the horizon in these four seasons will be as in Figures 83, 84, 85, and 86. The situation is reversed for the waning crescents. For example, in the autumn the crescent lies on its back in the morning, as does the waxing spring crescent in the evening.

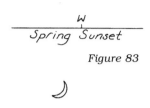

Spring Sunset

Figure 83

These are instructive items of observation for young students, as are the passages of the Sun at different times of year. And for the answers to the Moon's appearances, one returns to the Sun. Another example is the full Moon which, because it lies opposite to the Sun, (i.e., on the opposite side of the zodiac) always makes an opposite kind of movement. So, during the day the winter Sun will make a low arc across the sky, while the winter full Moon during the night will make a high arc (Figure 87).

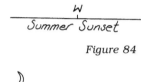

Summer Sunset

Figure 84

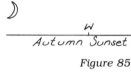

Autumn Sunset

Figure 85

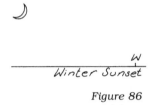

Winter Sunset

Figure 86

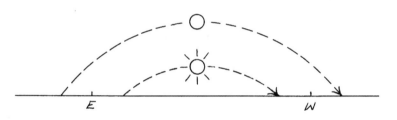

Figure 87

In summer the full Moon will make a low arc, while in spring and autumn the Sun and full Moon both move on the same arc (the celestial equator). Because the Moon when full, stands in the sky more or less as the Sun does in the opposite season and because the stars around the Moon are visible, when one looks at the full Moon one is seeing the equivalent of the Sun standing in a zodiacal constellation. For example, at midwinter the full Moon will represent the midsummer Sun in the stars of the Bull and Twins (Figure 88).

Figure 88

Another consequence of the full Moon's behavior is that its positions are likely to have been built into the layout of ancient stone circles. It is thought that Stonehenge, for example, was constructed to show, among other things, the positions of the rising and setting of Sun and Moon. In Figure 89 the circle is the horizon and, for one season, it is seen that Sun and full Moon do opposite things. Their positions switch round in mid-winter, while in autumn and spring they rise and set at the same places—due east and west. Figure 89 is simplified, the Moon varying its rising and setting points a little to left and right of the arrows over a number of years. The angle as shown between midsummer sunrise and mean midsummer moonrise for the latitude of Stonehenge is about 80 degrees. Sun and Moon had a special importance for people of earlier times, and their positions were well known and carefully recorded.

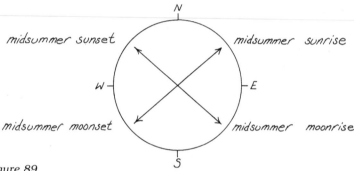

Figure 89

There are many references to the Moon in literature, some of them problematic ones. An example is Coleridge's description of the rising waning moon in "The Rime of the Ancient Mariner":

> Till clomb above the eastern bar
> The horned Moon, with one bright star
> Within the nether tip.

If Coleridge meant there was a star shining in the dark area within the arms of the crescent, then he was describing the impossible. Although one may only see a crescent shape, it is part of the sphere of the Moon which is nevertheless still there. A star (which must always be beyond the Moon) can only shine outside the complete circle of the Moon (Figure 90).

Figure 90

However, Coleridge may have been referring to a starlike phenomenon on the Moon which was reported to the Royal Society as "An Account of an Appearance of Light, like a Star, seen in the dark Part of the Moon, on Friday the 7th March, 1794"—a few years before "The Rime of the Ancient Mariner" was written. The astronomer William Herschel judged that the light's position on the Moon coincided with the crater Aristarchus.

If an ordinary star is within the circumference of the Moon's disc, it is hidden by the Moon, and this is called an occultation of the star. In fact, the part of the Moon outside the crescent is often seen glowing with a grey-blue "ashen" light, and a popular saying refers to the crescent as "the young moon with the old moon in its arms." The dim glow beyond the crescent is caused by reflected light from the *Earth* (earthshine). Like the Moon, the Earth also reflects light from the Sun into space.

Astronomical references in Shakespeare's works include act 2, scene 1 of Macbeth. The scene opens:

> (Enter Banquo, and Fleance, with a torch before him.)
> BANQUO: How goes the night, boy?
> FLEANCE: The moon is down; I have not heard the clock.
> BANQUO: And she goes down at twelve.
> FLEANCE: I take't, 'tis later, sir.
> BANQUO: Hold, take my sword. There's husbandry in
> heaven; Their candles are all out.

On a starless evening a bright phase of the Moon could shine through thin cloud or mist and still be seen before it sets. So Fleance could observe it "go down" or set. When King Duncan arrived at the castle earlier that evening, Banquo noted "This guest of summer, the temple-haunting martlet" or martin. So we can assume it was a summer night (the historical King Duncan was killed in battle on August 14, 1040). At midnight in summer the ecliptic would lie low across the horizon from east to west, and the Moon phase to "go down" at midnight is first quarter. It would set as in Figure 91.

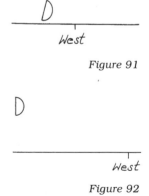

Figure 91

Figure 92

At sunset that evening, near when the King arrived at the beginning of act 1, scene 6, the Moon would have been "upright" and higher to the left (Figure 92).

So we know the phase of the Moon on the night King Duncan was murdered, and stage set designers may well use such information in depicting the sky above Macbeth's castle.

have no more than 12 complete lunar days. The Sun will rise in the lunar morning with a flash of light transforming night to day in a moment, because there is no atmosphere to create dawn. Sunset will quickly plunge the lunar landscape from day into night. During the day the Sun will shine in a black, starless sky, again because there is no atmosphere. But the Earth's atmosphere and oceans will cause the Earth to shine out in white and blue color.

Also, whatever phase the Moon appears at from Earth, the Earth will appear in the opposite (complementary) phase seen from the Moon. When we see a crescent Moon in the sky, the lunar inhabitant in the grey-blue ashen-light area (where it is night) will experience the Earth as gibbous. In fact, the shape of the ashen-lit area seen on the Moon from Earth is the shape of the Earth's phase seen at that moment from the Moon. So the crescent Moon with ashen light shows two realities in our sky.

Figure 95 shows the basic situation for a point on the lunar surface facing Earth. The far side of the Moon never experiences the Earth in the sky at all. Astronomy has provided writers with plenty of stranger-than-fiction circumstances for stories of other worlds.

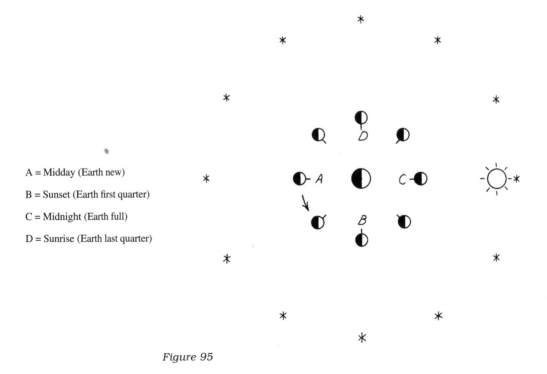

A = Midday (Earth new)

B = Sunset (Earth first quarter)

C = Midnight (Earth full)

D = Sunrise (Earth last quarter)

Figure 95

Supplementary Exercises

1.

A Moon calendar showing the approximate dates for Moon phases during a particular month can be made simply. Cut out two circular pieces of cardboard of different sizes. Divide the edge of the larger one into 30 equal parts of 12 degrees each. Number the divisions anticlockwise to represent dates (Figure 96), disregarding for the moment those months with 28, 29, or 31 days.

Divide the smaller disc into 12 equal parts and place a phase of the Moon at each, also proceeding anticlockwise, as in Figure 97.

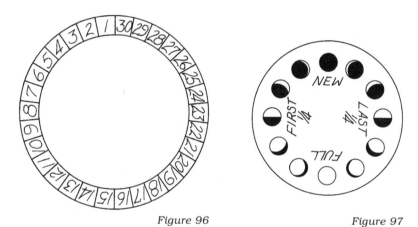

Figure 96   Figure 97

The smaller disc is placed on top of the larger, perhaps with a split pin to pass through their centers. Find the date of any phase (say new Moon) and place that phase beside that date. The other phases will then be indicated beside the dates when they occur during a lunar month. If a month has, say, 31 days, then an adjustment can be made at the end of the 30th day by moving the smaller disc back a day and counting 30 as 31. If the month has 28 days, then at the end of the 28th day the smaller disc can be moved forward two days. A month of 29 days should have the phase disc moved forward one day at the end of the 29th. This keeps the calendar close to the 29-1/2 day lunar month.

Astronomical calendars (see Appendix 5) give the dates of the main Moon phases for a particular year.

2.

The shape of a phase of the Moon can be constructed using the principle of plan and elevation. This has a connection with Figure 78. Figure 98 is a plan view when the Moon is 60 degrees east of the Sun, or about 5 days old—the smaller drawing showing the overall view.

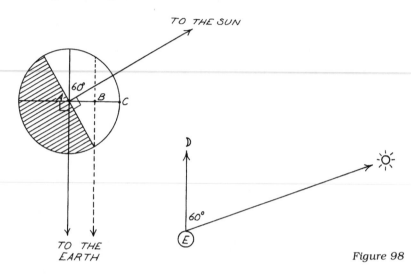

Figure 98

Point A in the larger drawing is the center of the Moon. The two vertical lines are parallel, and both point to the Earth since it is so far away. The broken line cuts off the width of lit surface seen by the observer on Earth—that is, the line BC.

Figure 99 shows the same proportions seen in elevation (that is, sideways) from the Earth. AB is the same length as in Figure 98.

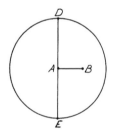

Figure 99

DBE now lies on the curve of the shadow edge (terminator) on the Moon. But three points are not enough to define this curve since many curves (including a circle) can be drawn through three points. The correct curve is part of an ellipse and can be found as follows (Figure 100).

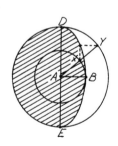

Figure 100

Using Figure 99, draw another circle with center A and radius AB. Draw a line from A cutting the circles at X and Y. From X draw a line parallel to DE, and from Y a line parallel to AB. Their point of intersection will lie on the required ellipse. Other points can be found with other lines through A. The crescent DBE/DYE is the shape of the 5-day-old Moon. The situation can be demonstrated by painting half of a table-tennis ball black and looking down on it as in Figure 98, with the arrows to Earth pointing toward you. Then rotate the top of the ball away from you so as to see it from the side; the appropriate phase of the Moon will be shown by the slice of white which you see.

On the actual surface of the Moon, the line DBE *is* a semicircle, but is being seen from Earth at an oblique angle. This transforms it into an ellipse, as the table-tennis ball shows. The ball can also show why, when the Moon is, say, halfway between new and first quarter, point B on the crescent is not half-way between A and C—and, therefore, why the lit area grows into the crescent phase slowly, passes through first quarter quickly, and reaches full slowly again. A little handling of the ball will make these phase phenomena clear.

For a simple exercise to teach younger students to draw a correct crescent (or gibbous) shape freehand, only Figure 99 need be constructed; point B can be chosen freely on a line through A at right angles to DE.

Chapter Five

Eclipses

When eclipses occur, either the Sun or the Moon becomes darkened, its shape changing and its lit area reducing in size as if it were going through phases within a short time.

Of the two types, lunar eclipses are the most frequently seen from any one location. They take place when the Moon is full, and, if the eclipse is total, the Moon is often seen to reduce to a dim disc in a clear sky, where only shortly before it had shone brilliantly.

Figure 101

Figure 101 shows the range of appearance the full Moon can take during a total eclipse. The process begins at position 1 on the left and goes to the right. This represents the Moon's diurnal motion, left to right, during the evening.

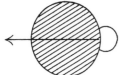

Figure 102

The reason for the change in shape is that the Moon is entering the Earth's shadow. With its own orbital (monthly eastward) motion round the Earth, the Moon is passing through the shadow from right to left (Figure 102). The Moon can remain totally eclipsed for almost 1-3/4 hours, during which it often takes on a reddish color due to the Earth's atmosphere filtering the Sun's light. The Earth's sunrise-sunset halo shines toward the Moon. From the moment the Moon begins to enter the Earth's shadow to the moment it leaves, can take around four hours.

Knowledge of a lunar eclipse saved Christopher Columbus and his men from disaster in the year 1504 during his fourth and last voyage. Two of his vessels, sinking from shipworm, sought refuge in St. Ann's Bay, Jamaica, where they were lashed together to keep them upright. Columbus was marooned there for a year before a rescue ship arrived, and he depended in the meantime on the island natives to provide food. But in February 1504 the natives refused to give any more food. Columbus knew from his astronomical tables that a total eclipse of the Moon was due on February 29. So he gathered the natives together that day and made a speech, telling them through an interpreter that he had come there at God's command. He said that God was very annoyed with them and would show his anger that night with signs in the heavens. The Moon was wholly within the Earth's shadow for 48 minutes in the early evening at Jamaica, during which it was "almost completely obscured." This was enough for the natives to change their minds and continue supplying Columbus and his men with food until they were rescued.

Incidentally, there is a popular idea that Columbus's first voyage westward to reach a land to the east established that the Earth was a sphere. But the Earth as a sphere had been taught by the Pythagoreans and by Aristotle, Ptolemy, Thomas Aquinas, Dante, and so on. In 1490 a commission under Queen Isabella of Castile, turning down Columbus's request for ships, said that there were no antipodes because the greater part of the globe was covered in water, as stated by St. Augustine. The commission judged that Columbus's plan rested on "weak foundations" which "appeared uncertain and impossible to any educated person, however little learning he might have." Further reasons for this included their opinion that the Western Ocean was perhaps unnavigable; that if he reached the antipodes he could not get back; that only three of the Earth's five "zones" were habitable; and that it was unlikely anyone could find unknown lands of any value so long after the Creation.

Columbus eventually set sail, knowing by experience what every navigator knew—that to travel north or south shifted the height of the northern stars above the horizon, which would happen if the Earth were a globe. This phenomenon had been Aristotle's proof that the Earth was a globe. Also, Ptolemy demonstrated that the Earth was not flat by showing that locations to the east or west of each other did not experience the same time—the more easterly places recorded an eclipse of the Moon (which happens at the same moment for all observers on Earth) as occurring at a later time of night. In the 13th century, Marco Polo had journeyed to the east and discovered India, China, and Japan, and Columbus was determined to reach these lands by sailing west.

Enlightened scepticism about Columbus's voyage with regard to the Earth's shape was probably more concerned with whether he would find land at the other side of the Earth with nature and people upside down instead of empty ocean, rather than with whether the Earth was a sphere. Some sections of the European population no doubt considered, on the evidence of their senses from one fixed location, that the Earth was flat, but those who were concerned with Columbus's voyage certainly knew the Earth to be a sphere, and the expedition was not undertaken to prove it. It had been established in thought, and proven empirically, long before. (Quotations above are taken from *Christopher Columbus* by John Stewart Collis; Readers Union, Newton Abbot, England, 1977.)

To return to our theme, eclipses of the Sun are seen less frequently from any one place on the Earth than are eclipses of the Moon. Also, the time during which the Sun is completely eclipsed is much less. In a total solar eclipse, day becomes night for a maximum of about 7-1/2 minutes, and bright stars and planets shine in the sky. Before and after that, the Sun goes through "phases" as in Figure 103, which are opposite to the shapes which the eclipsed Moon goes through (Figure 101).

Figure 103

The phases are caused by the Moon passing in front of the Sun (Figure 104).

Figure 104

The start of this movement of the Moon across the face of the Sun takes place at position 1 in Figure 103. The Sun then moves to the right (from east to west) above the horizon and the Moon moves further to the left across the Sun (monthly eastward motion) as in position 2, and so on. From the moment that the Moon first appears to touch the Sun to when it leaves can take a maximum of almost four hours.

During a solar eclipse the Sun must never be looked at directly, otherwise damage to the retina of the eye will result. Teachers can set up a pinhole camera with a cardboard box for viewing the eclipse on a tracing-paper screen (Figure 105).

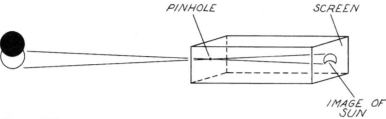

Figure 105

The image of the Sun on the screen will, of course, be inverted. Even a large pinhole in a piece of card will project an image of the Sun onto another white piece of card. A slide viewer with a lens which uses daylight, provides a ready-made camera obscura if the lens is held toward the Sun (but not at eye level). Binoculars or a small telescope can be used to project images of the Sun onto a white screen. Some amateur astronomers use arc-welder's glass as a filter through which to view the Sun without a telescope, and shade #14 has been recommended (*Sky & Telescope*, September 1989, p. 289). A safe filter can also be used to observe sunspots. Definitely not safe for viewing the Sun are sunglasses or, for example, glass darkened with candle smoke. The Sun must never be looked at without proper protection.

Figure 106 now gives a technical explanation for eclipses, with the observer removed into space. It can be seen from this diagram that only a small area on the surface of the Earth experiences a particular solar eclipse (the Moon's shadow casts a circle with a maximum diameter of about 250 kilometers when the Sun is overhead), but that about half of the Earth experiences a lunar eclipse.

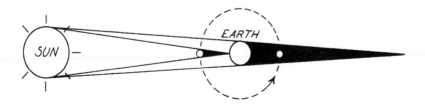

Figure 106

Figure 107

Figure 108

All eclipses are not total. In partial eclipses, the "phase" of greatest darkening is a kind of crescent. Figure 107 shows the case of a solar eclipse, and Figure 108 shows that of a lunar eclipse.

It will be noticed that the Sun and Moon have been drawn the same size, and on average this is almost exactly true. The "apparent" diameters of the Sun and Moon are approximately the same even though the Sun is physically larger, because the geometrical relationship between Sun, Moon and Earth is as shown in Figure 109.

Figure 109

Figure 110

There are times when the Moon is further away from the Earth than at others, and this causes its apparent diameter to become less than that of the Sun. If a solar eclipse occurs at this time, then the Moon cannot completely cover the disc of the Sun, and the result is an annular (or ring-shaped) eclipse (Figure 110).

Solar eclipses do not occur every month at new Moon, nor do lunar eclipses occur whenever there is a full Moon. The reason is that the path of the Moon in the sky is tilted at an angle of about five degrees to the path of the Sun, and eclipses can take place only about every six months near where their paths cross. In early times the eclipse areas were depicted as being under the rulership of a dragon (represented by the shadow of the Moon or the Earth), with the dragon's head at the place where the Moon crossed from below to above the path of the Sun, and the tail where it passed from above to below (Figure 111).

DRAGON'S TAIL

DRAGON'S HEAD

Figure 111

As indicated earlier, solar eclipses are rarer events from any particular place on Earth than lunar eclipses. This is especially so for total solar eclipses. The next total solar eclipse to take place in Britain will occur in Cornwall on August 11, 1999. The shadow of the Moon will then sweep eastward over Paris on its way across Europe, the Black Sea, Turkey, Iran, and India. The United States and Canada will experience their next total solar eclipse on August 21, 2017. However, North America will have an annular eclipse on May 10, 1994. Australia and New Zealand had an annular eclipse on January 16, 1991. Australia will next have an annular eclipse on February 16, 1999, and a total solar eclipse on December 4, 2002.

Many diaries give details of eclipses for a particular year, as do astronomical handbooks and calendars (see also Appendix 1).

Supplementary Exercise

The shapes of the Moon at the beginning and end of a total lunar eclipse can be easily drawn as in Figure 112. The diameter of the Earth's shadow (large shaded circle) at the Moon's distance is about 2-1/2 times the apparent diameter of the Moon.

Figure 113 illustrates three shapes of the Moon during a partial lunar eclipse.

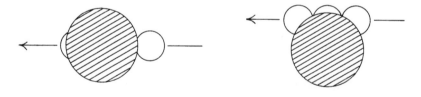

Figure 112   *Figure 113*

Chapter Six

The Planets

To unaided vision, the planets look like stars. The two things which distinguish them are their movements and, usually, their brightness. There is a popular saying that stars twinkle and planets do not, which is mostly true. Twinkling occurs because differing densities and temperatures within the Earth's upper atmosphere cause light to refract at varying angles. A star is a point source of light and is easily affected by this, but a planet has a disc with a diameter and the trembling rays are less noticeable.

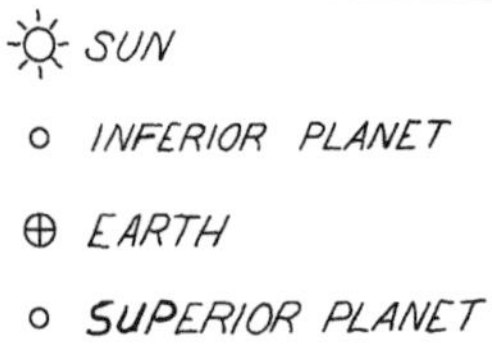

☼ *SUN*

o *INFERIOR PLANET*

⊕ *EARTH*

o *SUPERIOR PLANET*

Figure 114

Planets can be divided into two groups—inferior ones which are less distant from the Sun than the Earth and superior ones which are more distant from the Sun than the Earth (Figure 114). This particular difference in their positions gives them a completely dissimilar behavior as seen from Earth.

First, the inferior planets. These are Mercury and Venus. Seen from the Earth, they appear to oscillate to left and right of the Sun and, in principle, can be represented as in Figure 115.

Figure 115

Planets are not normally visible during the day, and Mercury and Venus can be seen when they have moved to left or right of the Sun and when the Sun is below the horizon (Figure 116). This means that they are morning stars in the east or evening stars in the west. The planet's two positions in Figure 116 are at opposite ends of its orbit, so that morning and evening appearances are separated in time.

Figure 116

Mercury and Venus will spend a certain period in which they are visible on these arcs above the Sun. During this time the Sun will move along the horizon from sunrise to sunrise or from sunset to sunset. In addition the ecliptic (to which the planets keep fairly close) will change its angle to the horizon. The combination of these factors results in the sort of movement for the planet in the evening shown theoretically in Figure 117.

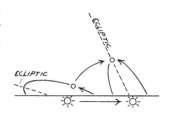

Figure 117

Venus moves further from the Sun and spends a longer time than Mercury does moving on its curve. It remains visible in the evening or morning sky for up to eight months. During this time the Sun and ecliptic alter their relationships to the horizon considerably (passing through about three seasons) so that the path which Venus traces is long and variously curved. Figure 118 gives an example of its path in the evening shortly after sunset from July to April at latitude 40 degrees north.

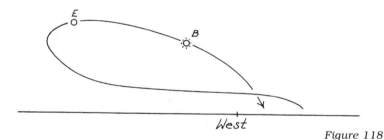

Figure 118

Position E in Figure 118 marks the planet's point of furthest distance from the Sun, called greatest elongation. For Venus to return to a greatest elongation in the evening sky takes just over 19 months. Between times it makes its appearance in the morning sky.

Venus is the brightest planet and at its evening appearance reaches "greatest brilliancy" toward the end of its path as it leaves the visible sky (position B in Figure 118). At its morning appearance it is brightest soon after entering the sky.

The path traced in Figure 118 is only one example of what shape of curve this planet can make above the horizon, plotted from night to night shortly after sunset. From year to year the curve alters, its form depending on the dates of the planet's appearance. The curve repeats its shape every 8 years (see Supplementary Exercises at the end of this chapter).

Mercury, by comparison, spends a very short time visibly apart from the Sun, varying from about one to three weeks in midnorthern latitudes. It moves quicker and is inside the path of Venus round the Sun. Altogether, its swift oscillation to left and right of the Sun carries it three complete times into the evening sky and three complete times into the morning sky in a year. During its brief appearances, the Sun and ecliptic move little in relation to the horizon, so Mercury's curve is mainly due to its own dynamic movement. The steep angle of the ecliptic to the horizon on spring evenings and autumn mornings (Figure 119) places Mercury in favorable positions for viewing when visible at these times. However, Mercury's small elongation from the Sun in spring and autumn, and its varying dates of elongation, can make other times favorable too.

Figure 119

A generalized picture of sequential appearances of Mercury in the course of the year, before sunrise and after sunset, is shown in Figure 120.

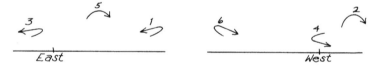

Figure 120

The translation of an old Babylonian word for Mercury is "jumping." The planet appears in the sky about every two months, alternating between west and east, between evening and morning. It actually enters the sky seven times in the course of a calendar year, but seven curves are not completed within the 12 months. Seen from Earth, it makes a circuit of the sun (e.g., from the greatest elongation east and back to there again) in about 116 days (synodic period).

Mercury is opposite in behavior to Venus in several ways, two of them being speed and brightness. Venus is splendid in its white brilliance, dominating the evening or morning scene, while Mercury is shy and faint and often difficult to identify. Also, Mercury, unlike Venus, is at its greatest brilliancy at the *beginning* of its curve in the *evening* sky (before greatest elongation) and at the *end* of its curve in the *morning* sky (after greatest elongation).

The superior planets Mars, Jupiter, and Saturn present quite a different picture to the observer than do the inferior ones. The superior planets are not harnessed so closely to the Sun or to the evening and morning skies. They certainly appear in those places along with Venus and Mercury, but unlike them they pass completely out of the morning sky, back toward midnight and evening. In other words, in the morning they rise earlier and earlier, moving westward in relation to the Sun from day to day and week to week (Figure 121).

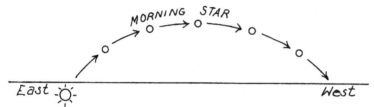

Figure 121

This takes them beyond the limits of the curves of Venus and Mercury in the morning, and they can reach the midnight sky opposite the Sun. In fact, a superior planet is at its brightest when it sets at sunrise, and thus rises at sunset and is due south at midnight (Figure 122). The planet in Figure 122 is said to be in "opposition" to the Sun.

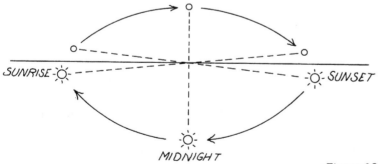

Figure 122

After the superior planet rises at sunset, it officially enters the evening sky and continues its westward movement week by week, this time toward the Sun, until it becomes swallowed up in the light of sunset (Figure 123).

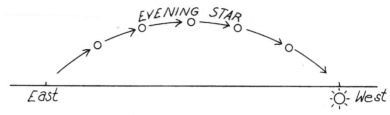

Figure 123

Mars spends about a year as an evening or morning star. Jupiter, which is further out in its orbit, is an evening or morning star for about 6 months. Saturn is further out still and shines in morning or evening for a little less time than does Jupiter.

The foregoing is the superior planets' relation to the Sun and the horizon. In relation to the background of stars, their movements are more varied. Like Mercury and Venus, they make curves. In fact, they mostly make loops (Figure 124).

Figure 124

The superior planets are at opposition and are brightest in the middle of a loop, at the position marked in Figure 124. For most of the time, these planets move from right to left (eastward) against the stars, but periodically they slow down, turn, and produce a loop or similar figure. The geometrical reason for this is given in the next chapter. For the moment it is important that the observed phenomena, out of which theory later arises, are grasped in their original forms. Too rapid a switch to theory can draw attention away from what is actually experienced in nature. The fact that a planet can be seen to make such a loop is extraordinary enough in itself and should be pondered on for a while. These apparent movements are the result of the planets' relationship to the Earth and are no less a signature of their characteristics than are the theoretical ones.

For the Earth observer under the night sky, Mars comes into opposition to the Sun about every 2 years and 7 weeks, at which time it is making a loop, taking about 2-1/3 months to move backward (retrograde) in the loop against the stars. Jupiter makes a loop every year, spending about 4 months in retrograde motion. Saturn also makes a yearly loop, but spends longer in the retrograde part of it, about 4-1/2 months. The further out the planets are, the slower they move, and the smaller are their loops. This describes the situation for the watchful observer of any age—thousands of years ago or now.

Supplementary Exercises

The rhythms of planets' appearances can be recorded in simple diagrams on circular pieces of cardboard and kept for future reference. We can choose Venus as an inferior planet and Mars as a superior one. What is shown here is their synodic periods, that is, the time that elapses between repetitions of the same relationship to Sun and Earth. For instance, a synodic period extends from Venus's appearance as an evening star at greatest elongation east, to its reappearance in that position (on average 19.2 months later).

Figure 125

Using this period of Venus, it is seen that 19.2 months carries it round the zodiac once plus 3/5ths of the circle (Figure 125). This is because it stands in the same relation to the Sun at the beginning and end of that time, and the Sun takes 12 months to complete the circle.

EVENING ELONGATIONS OF VENUS

Figure 126

When this period repeats 5 times, Venus will have its greatest elongations east almost exactly at the place it started from 8 years earlier. So we can use two pentagrams to mark a series of greatest elongations east and west (Figures 126 and 127).

Mars reaches oppositions (when it is brightest and rises at sunset) at average intervals of 2.13 years apart, and in this time moves anticlockwise round the zodiac once plus about 1/7th of the circle. So in roughly 15 years it will have 8 oppositions placed round the zodiac including its return to near its starting point, 7 of them represented here by a heptagon (Figure 128).

MORNING ELONGATIONS OF VENUS

Figure 127

In addition to keeping a record of dates, these diagrams retain something of the geometrical signature of these planets in their appearance in the zodiac as related to Earth.

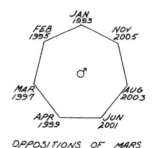

OPPOSITIONS OF MARS

Figure 128

Chapter Seven

The Copernican Revolution

And new Philosophy calls all in doubt,
The Element of fire is quite put out;
The Sun is lost, and th' earth, and no man's wit
Can well direct him where to looke for it.

So wrote the English poet John Donne in the early 1600s when the movement of the Earth was still a matter of controversy. Donne was uneasy about the effect which the idea of the Earth's movement would have on humanity's picture of the heavens. Yet the arguments for and against the Earth's movement were both idealistic in their ways—the motionless Earth concept allowing the heavens to retain their mysterious, spiritual quality in their turning round the Earth in magnificent spheres; the moving-Earth idea marking a triumph in rational thinking. The first view was faithful to direct observational experience; the second added the bright jewel of abstract thought. As human experiences, they do not contradict but complement each other. One view is true to the Earth observer's immediate experience, the other to the human's geometrical mind, which moves the Earth in space whether this is supported by direct experience or not. To move the Earth, we *see* the Sun rising but *think* the Earth to be rotating on its axis; or we *see* the stars in the south from midnight to midnight shifting from left to right but *think* the Earth to be orbiting from right to left and round the hidden Sun in the north behind us.

Figure 129 shows an old Earth-centered system that includes the Sun and Moon as planets. Their ordering can be arrived at by measuring their average daily motion eastward (right to left) against the stars—the Moon moving fastest and therefore considered closest to the Earth; Saturn moving slowest and considered furthest. The Moon has a mean motion eastward of about 13.18 degrees a day, Mercury 1.4 degrees, Venus 1.2 degrees, the Sun .98 degrees, Mars .75 degrees, Jupiter .2 degrees, and Saturn .08 degrees. Seen from the Earth, the approximate times taken by the superior planets to make one circuit of the zodiac are Saturn 29-1/2 years, Jupiter 12 years, and Mars 2 years. The Sun takes 1 year. Venus can overtake the Sun and therefore can be considered quicker and nearer the Earth; Mercury overtakes the Sun quicker still; and the Moon overtakes it quickest of all, making one circuit of the zodiac in about 27.32 days.

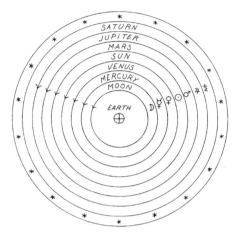

Figure 129

A mind deeply stirred by the alternative idea of the Sun as center of the planetary orbits was that of Nicolaus Copernicus, who was born in 1473 in Torun, a Prussian town then under Polish rule, on the river Vistula. Figure 130 shows the basis of his system, with the Earth as one of the planets, carrying its moon along with it. It should be noted that the old Earth-centered ordering of the planets places Mercury closer to the Earth than Venus while the new Copernican ordering places Venus closer to the Earth than Mercury. Mercury being closer to us is correct for the old "time" positioning (daily sidereal eastward movement), while Venus being closer to us is correct for the "space" positioning of Copernicus.

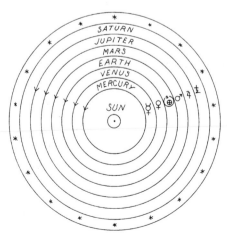

Figure 130

THE COPERNICAN REVOLUTION   67

In the modern Sun-centered system, Mercury is calculated to make one orbit round the Sun (seen against the background of the stars) in 87.97 days, Venus in 224.70 days, Earth in 365.26 days, Mars in 686.98 days, Jupiter in 11.86 years, Saturn in 29.46 years, Uranus in 84.01 years, Neptune in 164.79 years, and Pluto in 247.69 years.

Copernicus was the youngest of four children of a merchant who died when the boy was 10 years of age. After his father's death he was brought up by his uncle, Lucas Waczenrode, a Catholic bishop and scholar. This background eventually led to Copernicus' becoming Canon of Frombork Cathedral, not far from Gdansk, on the Baltic Sea, in what was then part of Polish Prussia. But by that time Copernicus had received a very wide education, having studied the classics, sciences (including medicine), and canon law at the universities of Cracow, Bologna, and Padua; two of his particular interests were mathematics and astronomy. His earliest reported observation was made in the year 1497, on March 9, when he carefully timed the moment when the Moon passed in front of and obscured the star Aldebaran. During a year's stay in Rome he recorded the partial lunar eclipse on the night of November 5 and 6, 1500.

When Copernicus became Canon at Frombork, he lived in one of the turrets in the fortified wall of the cathedral. The adjacent platform at the top of the wall could have served as an observatory; in any event, he noted more than 50 observations, both officially and on the margins and flyleaves of books, etc. One of the observations from the cathedral was the "opposition" of Mars on June 5, 1512 (the precise opposition was a day earlier, which may have been cloudy).

Even so, it was not astronomical observation but theory and ideas which fired him and in which he excelled. At about the time of his Mars observation, he wrote a short text called *Little Commentary* and circulated written copies among friends. This book was never published in his lifetime, but if it had been it would have created a great stir. It was a description of an unusual view of the universe: "All the spheres revolve about the Sun as their mid-point, and therefore the Sun is the center of the universe. . . . Whatever motion appears in the firmament arises not from any motion of the firmament, but from the Earth's motion."

Just as Columbus had, while Copernicus was a student at Cracow University, discovered a new world with his ships, so the astronomer was now discovering another new world with his mind. But Copernicus was reticent to reveal his findings to society at large and for many years refused to publish them. The insistence of friends, however, persuaded him to publish a complete mathematical account of the Sun-centered universe called *On The Revolutions of the Heavenly Spheres*, the first copy of which, according to a friend, reached Copernicus "only at his last breath upon the day that he died," on May 24, 1543. But many days before that special moment, he had "sadly lost his memory and mental vigor."

PLATE 6
Part of the defensive walls of Frombork Cathedral, situated in Polish Prussia at the time of Copernicus. The "Copernicus Tower" is on the right.
From *Land of Nicholas Copernicus* by Michal Rusinek; Twayne Publishers, New York, 1973.

Though it was a bold notion to develop, Copernicus's basic theory was not a new one to astronomers and historians. He himself had read or heard of theories which moved the Earth in space, taught by the Greeks who lived hundreds of years before him—for example, Aristarchus of Samos, who lived from about 310 to 230 B.C. Another whom he knew of was Philolaus (5th century B.C.), a follower of the philosophy of Pythagoras. This latter school of thought believed in keeping certain truths secret and only passing them on to followers by word of mouth. Copernicus's reticence to publish seems to have arisen out of a resurgence of such Pythagorean feelings, as he himself indicated in his book's dedication to Pope Paul III: "...I hesitated for a long time whether to bring my treatise, written to demonstrate its [the Earth's] motion, into the light of day, or whether it would not be better to follow the example of the Pythagoreans and certain others, who used to pass on the mysteries of their philosophy merely to their relatives and friends, not in writing but by personal contact...." He also predicted in the Preface that certain people would, on publication, "clamor for me to be hooted off the stage...."

In the first part of the text itself, Copernicus gives a lyrical and well-nigh religious description of his system: "In the middle of all is the seat of the Sun. For who in this most beautiful of temples would put this lamp in any other or better place than the one from which it can illuminate everything at the same time? Aptly indeed is he named by some the lantern of the universe, by others the mind, by others the ruler. Trismegistus called him the visible God, Sophocles' Electra, the watcher over all things. Thus indeed the Sun as if seated on a royal throne governs his household of Stars as they circle round him."

Space is here spent on detailing something of the life and ideas of Copernicus because the change he brought was momentous for human history and is one of the greatest of turning points. Too often his name simply means the audacious inventor of six irreligious circles drawn round the Sun, such circles being obvious today to anyone with common sense. But they are not obvious at all.

It has been emphasized that Copernicus's system was very much a theory in his mind, for he himself could not prove it by observation. In fact, Europe virtually believed in (or assumed by the calculation of solar system masses) the Copernican system before the first "observational" evidence came in the 18th century (James Bradley's telescopic determination in 1729 of the aberration of starlight caused by the earth's orbital motion). But there were many critics of the Sun-centered system before then. Martin Luther said of Copernicus; "The fool will turn the whole science of Astronomy upside down. But, as Holy Writ declares, it was the Sun and not the Earth which Joshua commanded to stand still." This was stated even before the publication of Copernicus's book.

A more understanding and elegant counter to Copernicus's system was given by the great Danish astronomer Tycho Brahe (1546-1601). Brahe, an unsurpassed and accurate observer of the heavens, built the world's first professional observatory (in the modern scientific sense) on the little Danish island of Hveen. A nobleman, he was financially supported in this by King Frederick II of Denmark. With his instruments, before the invention of the telescope, he could find no shift in the positions of the stars which would result if the Earth were moving round the Sun. Such a shift is called annual parallax.

The Greek philosopher Aristotle (384–322 B.C.) said that if the Earth were in orbital motion, the apparent position of each star would reciprocally move back and forth. A geometric principle which could be employed in detecting annual parallax, and is thought to have been used by Copernicus, is illustrated in Figure 131.

Figure 131

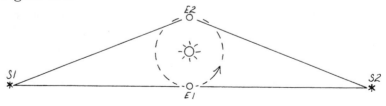

Two stars are chosen (S1 and S2) in principle 180 degrees apart when the Earth is at position E1. Six months later at E2 the positions of the stars are measured again when any angle less than 180 degrees between the lines E2, S1 and E2, S2 would indicate a shift in their apparent positions on the celestial sphere. But neither Copernicus nor Tycho Brahe detected any parallactic shift, whatever method they used. Brahe tried in vain to find an annual parallax for the Pole Star. The great Italian scientist Galileo (1564-1642) suggested a method, which is to measure the apparent distance between two stars near each other on the celestial sphere, but hopefully at different distances from the Earth. Measurements made six months apart would reveal, if the Earth moved, the two stars to shift in relation to each other as a reflection of the Earth's orbit (Figure 132). The nearer star would have the larger annual parallax on the celestial sphere. But the first certain measurement of this movement was not achieved until 1838 when the German astronomer Friedrich Bessel detected with a telescope a minute shift (corresponding to the diameter of a coin seen from several kilometers away) in the position of the faint star 61 Cygni (constellation of the Swan) compared with two stars nearby on the celestial sphere.

PLATE 9

Galileo (Galileo Galilei). Frontispiece portrait to his book *Il Saggiatore* (*The Assayer*), 1623.

From *Watchers of the Stars*, by Patrick Moore; Michael Joseph Publishers, 1974.

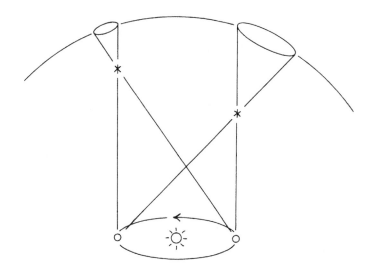

Figure 132

Because all the stars are so very distant, Tycho Brahe could never have detected such tiny movements as these with his early instruments, wonderfully precise though they were for his time.

Though Tycho Brahe had no evidence for, and did not believe in, the movement of the Earth, he admired much of Copernicus's work and so came to a compromise, devising an interesting system which could fit with a new theory of the planets and also with the old view of the Earth standing still. He made the planets move round the Sun, but the Sun, Moon, and stars move round the Earth (Figure 133). Mathematically this planetary system is exactly equivalent to the Sun-centered one. He made the orbit of Mars cross that of the Sun (though geometrically the two cannot collide with each other) because he calculated that at one stage in its orbit (opposition) Mars came closer to the Earth than the Sun. Brahe was a vigorous, honest thinker who nevertheless found himself caught between the old and the new, and devised a system which allowed past and present to live in harmony.

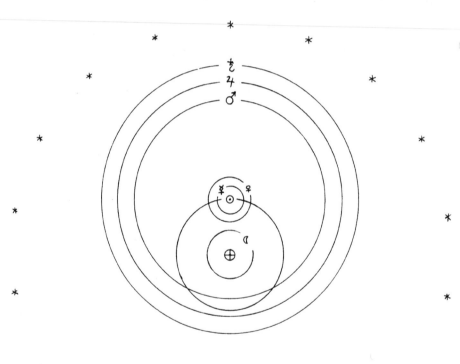

Figure 133

Despite his great scientific mind, Brahe could be idiosyncratic and cantankerous in his relationships with people. When he was 20 and a guest at a Christmas party in Rostock in Germany, he quarreled with a Danish nobleman, and they fought a duel with swords at 7 o' clock in the evening in the dark. Brahe had part of his nose cut off and after that wore a replacement made of a mixture of gold and silver. The combatants were said to have become good friends afterward.

The Danish astronomer eventually left his island of Hveen and continued his work in Bohemia, where the Emperor Rudolf II gave him a castle in Benatky, not far from Prague. The great German astronomer Johannes Kepler (1571–1630) travelled to Benatky to meet Brahe and there followed a collaboration between them (not without difficulty, for both were strong individuals with easily roused feelings) which brought as important a change in the science of astronomy as had the work of Copernicus. Less than two years after their meeting, Tycho Brahe died, but not before Kepler had become acquainted with Brahe's wonderfully accurate observations of the planets, observations which later led Kepler to discover that Mars (and, consequently, the other planets) moved in ellipses round the Sun. Kepler's eyesight was poor (he could never have made Brahe's observations himself), but his imagination and his mathematics were supreme, and the combined talents of these two great men won the day.

PLATE 10
Johannes Kepler. Frontispiece portrait to *The Rudolphine Tables*, Ulm, 1627.
From *Watchers of the Stars*, by Patrick Moore; Michael Joseph Publishers, 1974.

Earlier geometry for the movements of the planets was based on circles, since these were considered appropriate to celestial bodies, the circle and sphere being thought more perfect than other figures. At Alexandria, the Greek center of learning about 2000 years ago, a simplified version of the Sun's apparent movement round the zodiac placed it on a circle which was eccentric (off-center) to the Earth (Figure 134).

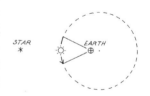

Figure 134

Seen from Earth, this made the Sun appear to move more swiftly against the stars when nearest to the Earth. This corresponds to observation; the Sun actually does appear to be closer (it looks larger) and move faster in January every year.

The innovation of Copernicus was simply to switch the positions of Earth and Sun; the effect seen from the Earth is the same (Figure 135).

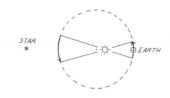

Figure 135

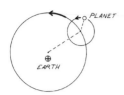

Figure 136

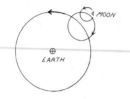

Figure 137

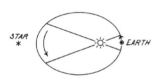

Figure 138

Figure 139

To represent more complicated movements of planets, the Greeks used the epicycle (a circle with its center standing on the circumference of another circle) as in Figure 136.

Copernicus also used epicycles in his system—a great many of them in fact. Figure 137 indicates his construction for the movement of the Moon.

But the mathematical genius of Kepler swept away eccentric circles and epicycles and replaced them with the elegant beauty and precision of the ellipse. For a planet's orbit, the sun was placed at one of the foci, the curve being exaggerated for clarity in Figure 138.

Kepler wrestled for years in Prague to reach this answer by long, intricate calculations, using Tycho Brahe's tables of the positions of Mars. First he progressed from a supposed circular orbit to an oval one. Shortly after Easter 1605, he suddenly realized that the curve was an ellipse, having the properties of an earlier drawing in which a line through the Sun from the planet swept out equal areas in equal times (areas shaded in Figure 139). He had discovered the geometrical secret of the solar system. "I felt as if I had awakened from a long sleep and were blinking at the bright sunlight," he wrote. At the time, Kepler was financially supported by Emperor Rudolf II, and said in a letter to him announcing his triumph over his adversary, Mars, the "god of war": "I bring to Your Majesty a noble prisoner whom I have captured in the difficult and wearisome war entered upon under Your auspices.... Arithmetic and Geometry brought him without resistance to our camp." In order to be able to continue his work with the other planets, Kepler added: "Yet, I beseech Your Majesty to remember that money is the sinew of war, and to have the bounty to order Your treasurer to deliver up to Your general the sums necessary for raising fresh troops." His appeal, as it happens, went unheeded, though the form it took demonstrated Kepler's lively imagination, which was his great asset as a scientist and led to so many of his discoveries in mathematics and astronomy.

Before discovering the elliptical orbits of the planets, Kepler's geometrical imagination brought him to a picture of the five Platonic solids (Figure 140) fitting between the orbits of the planets.

Each solid must be thought of as having an "insphere" or sphere touching the insides of its faces. Into this sphere is placed another solid with its corners on the sphere. The solids are nested in this way in the sequence, from largest to smallest—cube, tetrahedron, dodecahedron, icosahedron, octahedron. The Sun is at the center, enclosed lastly by the octahedron. The spheres will then relate to the planets, Mercury moving on its orbit inside the octahedron's insphere, Venus inside the icosahedron's, Earth inside the dodecahedron's, Mars inside the tetrahedron's, Jupiter inside the cube's, and Saturn near the biggest sphere which passes through the corners of the cube.

Kepler had his inspiration for a geometric relation between the orbits of the planets while teaching a mathematics class at the Protestant school in Graz, Styria, in July 1595. As in Figure 141, he drew an outer circle representing the zodiac and demonstrated the conjunctions of Jupiter and Saturn round it by connecting consecutive conjunctions with straight lines forming near-triangles. Conjunctions between these two planets occur about every 20 years and are about 117 degrees apart. There are 40 conjunction points round the outer circle and if consecutive conjunctions are connected (13 "steps" apart around the circle) 40 times, then one returns to where one started and the lines are tangents to an inner circle. During his class Kepler suddenly saw that the ratio between the outer and inner circles looked the same as the ratio between the orbits of Saturn and Jupiter. (This was close to the ratio of a cube's "circumsphere"—the sphere touching its corners—to its insphere, which ratio is the square root of 3 to 1. These two spheres are also referred to as "circumscribed" and "inscribed," respectively.) After no success with fitting a series of plane figures between the orbits of the planets, Kepler turned his mind to three dimensions and his Platonic solids theory of planetary distances was born.

The solids in Figure 140 are not shown nested inside each other since the proportions of the solar system are such that they would rapidly diminish in size, making the octahedron a very tiny shape at the center of the cube. The fit with the planetary orbits is surprisingly good, and Kepler felt it was significant, saying that, with this Platonic-solids scheme, "...you will have an answer for the peasant who asks what hooks the

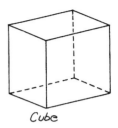

Cube

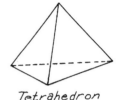

Tetrahedron

Dodecahedron

Icosahedron

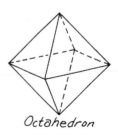

Octahedron

Figure 140

sky is hung on to prevent it from falling." Further details of Kepler's arrangement are given in a Note at the end of this chapter.

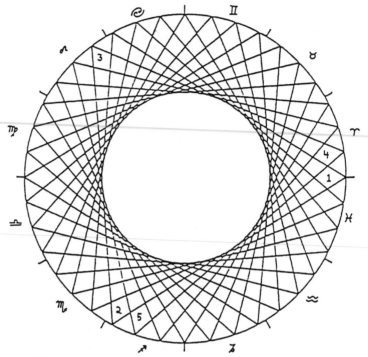

Figure 141

After his discovery of the planetary ellipses, Kepler saw in them a flower of intellectual and spiritual expression, relating the periods of the planets and their varying speeds on their ellipses to the "music of the spheres." Each planet had tones which varied with its speed (fast when near the Sun), Saturn's lowest note being the G next below the bottom of a modern piano keyboard, and Mercury's highest note the E next above a modern piano's keyboard—a range approaching the limits of human hearing. In elaborating this idea, Kepler remarked, "...I climb along the harmonic scale of the celestial movements to higher things where the true archetype of the fabric of the world is kept hidden." John Rodgers and Willie Ruff, two professors at Yale University's School of Music have represented these planetary harmonies on phonograph record, reducing the time scale such that 5 seconds represents one year, and choosing as a starting point the positions of the planets at Kepler's birth on December 27, 1571. The result, it should be said, is not a very "classical" sound, but rather a modern symphony of wails, thumps, and whistles.

The simple ellipse of Kepler leads to our modern geometrical picture of the solar system. It should be noted that the Earth's ellipse is so slight that, if drawn in pencil on a page, it would look like a circle, deviating from circularity by less than the thickness of the pencil line. Mathematically, the "eccentricity" (deviation from a circle) of the Earth's orbit is 0.017. Such was the subtlety of Tycho Brahe's and Kepler's work. Perhaps the ancients, who strove to have the planets move on circles, would not be displeased to know the truth. In any case, a circle is an ellipse with the two foci coinciding. Figure 142 shows the orbits of the naked-eye planets and Earth drawn to scale. The circles for Mercury, Mars, Jupiter, and Saturn have their centers displaced from the center of the Sun to represent their elliptical orbits. Circles with their centers displaced from the Sun or its center are correct as far as graphical geometry allows, as was known by the ancients. It is the clear eye of mathematics which perceives ellipses.

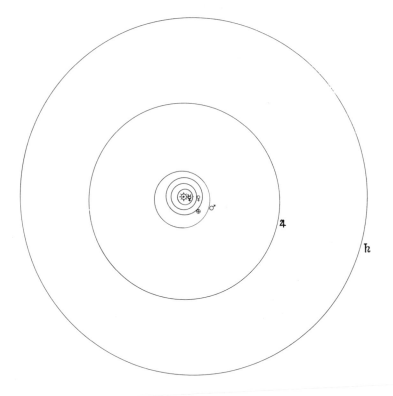

Figure 142

From *The Paths of the Planets*, by R.A.R. Tricker; Mills and Boon, London, 1967.

Concentric circles can be drawn for classroom demonstration of the comparative sizes of the orbits. If Sun to Earth is one unit, then, roughly, Sun to Mercury will be 0.4, to Venus 0.7, to Mars 1.5, to Jupiter 5.2, and to Saturn 9.5.

Certainly the ellipse was a great improvement on epicycles. In fact, Copernicus's system, though it was a momentous step in the realm of ideas, was no less complicated than the popular Earth-centered one of Ptolemy of Alexandria (2nd century A.D.). Copernicus's complete solar system model employed 48 circles. Often fewer were employed by 15th-century users of Ptolemy's system. Also, Copernicus's system was no more accurate than Ptolemy's.

Ptolemy's system had deeply influenced Western civilization for over a thousand years, and within the field of Earth-centered astronomy it was unsurpassed. The system was set out in detail in Ptolemy's book *Almagest* (Arabic: "The Greatest," to distinguish it from another work called *The Little Astronomer*). Not much is known about the author's life, but an Arabic text says: "He was of modest height and pale complexion, sturdily built and with an easy gait. He had a red birthmark on his left cheek and a luxuriant black beard. Though he was gap-toothed and small-mouthed, he showed great elegance of expression and pungency of logic. He was irascible to the point of implacability. His hobbies were walking and riding. He had a small appetite and indeed often fasted. His breath was sweet and he kept a well-laundered wardrobe. He died in his 78th year."

A comparison of the old system of the *Almagest* with the new reveals that in one important aspect Copernicus was more elegant and satisfying to the mind—in the geometry for the loops of the planets. This required not another epicycle but only the movement of the Earth, reflected in a planet's loop against the stars (simplified in Figure 143).

Seen from the Sun, the orbit of Mars is outside that of the Earth. Both move in the same direction (anticlockwise viewed from the north), and Mars, being furthest out, moves slowest. Therefore the Earth periodically overtakes Mars, causing the planet's movement seen from Earth against the stars to stop, move back (retrograde) to the right, and form a loop. The movement against the stars is not back and forward on a straight line since the orbits of Earth and Mars are tilted at an angle to each other, and the plane of Mars is not seen edge-on. As can be seen in Figure 143, Mars is closest to the Earth at position 4, and this causes it to appear brightest.

PLATE 11
Ptolemy (Claudius Ptolemaeus).

From *Great Astronomers*, by Robert Ball; Isbister and Company, London, 1895.

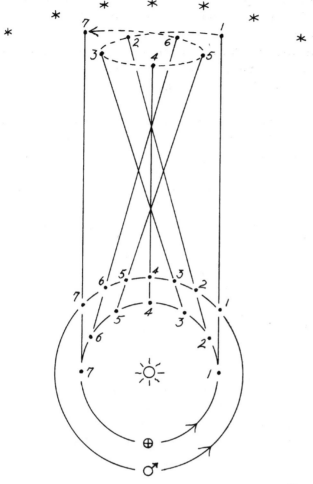

Figure 143

This explains the loop in Figure 124 of the last chapter and in reaching the explanation, a vitally important episode in science and human thinking has been surveyed.

Lastly, the modern astronomer calculates that not only does the Earth move in space, but the stars also have their individual "proper" motions in different directions, though these are so slow seen from our distance to them that the pattern of the constellations is changed only over many thousands of years. The first announcement of proper motion came from Edmond Halley in 1718 (shortly before he became England's Astronomer Royal), who compared the positions of Arcturus, Procyon, and Sirius with those given in Ptolemy's

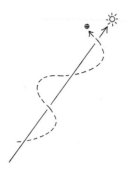

Figure 144

star catalogue hundreds of years earlier. Today our Sun is included as a star with its own motion in space—calculated to be moving toward a point in the constellation of Hercules, not far from the star Vega. The Sun carries our planets with it, and a diagrammatic view of this shows the Earth spiralling round the Sun in space (Figure 144).

This chapter can be closed and brought back to Earth with the observation that such a spiral motion can be found in many aspects of fluid and growth forms—for example in the way successive leaves wind their way up and round the stalks of plants. The Earth's spiral in space, imperceptible to ordinary vision, perhaps complements the obvious naked-eye spiralling of the Sun round the Earth from season to season as shown in Figure 46, Chapter 3.

Supplementary Exercises

1.

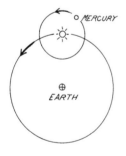

Figure 145

A simplified representation of an early epicyclic system can easily be constructed for, say, Mercury's apparent movement. Mercury is in the middle of a loop about every 116 days (synodic period); therefore in one year it will have made just over three loops as seen from Earth against the stars. Complete loops are not visible to the naked eye for this planet, because when it is in the middle of one it is in conjunction with (standing beside) the Sun, but theory allows us to calculate what occurs on the celestial sphere. For a general picture, draw a large circle to represent the course of the Sun round the Earth in a year, and a smaller one with its center at the Sun for the orbit of Mercury (Figure 145).

Taking Mercury's synodic period to be just under one-third of a year, divide the large circle into 20 equal parts, and the smaller into 6 equal parts. One must now imagine the planet to be moving round one-sixth of the smaller circle while the center of this circle moves round the circumference of the larger one by one-twentieth. The result will be that the planet performs a loop, shown in principle in Figure 146.

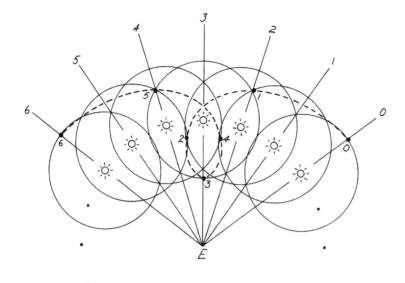

Figure 146

The measurement of one-sixth round the small circle can easily be done in steps with compasses set at the small circle's radius. The radial lines through the center E of the large circle make counting easier. For example, the radial line 0 cuts the first small circle at the planet's starting position 0. The planet's position at 1 is found by stepping with compasses one-sixth of the next small circle from its top point where it is cut by radial line 1, and so on. Position 3 on each small circle is already marked by where a radial line through its center cuts it, as with position 0. A division of the large circle into 40 and the small one into 12, will plot the loop in more detail.

It can be seen from this drawing that when Mercury is at position 0 it is beyond the Sun and in line with the Earth and Sun (superior conjunction); when at position 2 it is near elongation east (evening star); when at position 3 it is again in line with the Sun and Earth but now between them (inferior conjunction); when at position 4 it is near elongation west (morning star); and when at position 6 it returns to superior conjunction. For a time between positions 2 and 4 the planet is in retrograde (backward) motion from left to right.

2.

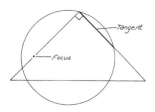

Figure 147

Turning to a Sun-centered movement for the planets, a simple ellipse can be drawn using an envelope of lines. Draw a circle and choose a point inside it near the circumference as the focus. Align a setsquare so that the right-angled corner lies on the circumference of the circle and one edge of the right angle lies on the focus. Then a line drawn along the other edge of the right angle is a tangent to an ellipse (Figure 147).

Drawing many cases of such tangents with this focus, produces an envelope to the ellipse, as in Figure 148. The extremities of the ellipse (perihelion and aphelion for a planet) touch the circle, where the tangent to the ellipse is also a tangent to the circle.

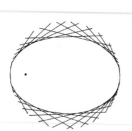

Figure 148

Notes on Planetary Distances

A. The Titius-Bode Law

Mention should be made of a remarkable number relationship in the distances of the planets from the Sun. It is called the Titius-Bode Law (sometimes just known as Bode's Law) and has a connection with the discovery of the minor planets or asteroids orbiting between Mars and Jupiter.

The law was first formulated in 1764 by the mathematician and physicist Johann Titius of Wittenberg, who inserted it as a new paragraph in his translation into German of a book (*Contemplation de la Nature*) by the French natural philosopher Charles Bonnet. The paragraph deals with the distances of the planets from the Sun in units and, in effect, states:

Mercury		4 units
Venus	4 + 3 =	7 units
Earth	4 + 6 =	10 units
Mars	4 + 12 =	16 units
?	4 + 24 =	28 units
Jupiter	4 + 48 =	52 units
Saturn	4 + 96 =	100 units

TABLE 1

As we can see, the number added to 4 is systematically doubled, and the result is remarkably close to the distances in "astronomical units" used earlier in the paragraph following Figure 142. One simply converts the answers to astronomical units by moving one decimal place back in each case, the Earth then becoming 1 unit from the Sun.

When he reached the gap between Mars and Jupiter, Titius wrote: "But see, from Mars and Jupiter there comes forth a departure from this so exact progression.... And shall the Builder have left this place empty? Never! Let us confidently wager that, without doubt, this place belongs to the as yet still undiscovered satellites of Mars."

Filling the gap with satellites of Mars was not a fruitful idea, but the rest was. The paragraph was read by the German mathematician and astronomer Johann Bode (1749-1826), who inserted the law as a footnote to a book he was writing on astronomy, *Anleitung zur Kenntniss des gestirnten Himmels*, and echoed Titius over the Mars-Jupiter gap with the words: "Can one believe that the Creator of the Universe has left this position empty? Certainly not."

Then in 1781 William Herschel in England discovered the planet Uranus with his telescope. The Titius-Bode Law placed this new planet at 19.6 astronomical units from the Sun, and this was close to the calculated distance. It was then Bode who gave the planet its name.

In 1800 Baron Francis von Zach, the court astronomer at Gotha, began arrangements for looking for a new planet between Mars and Jupiter by dividing the zodiac into 24 areas and assigning 24 astronomers one area each to search. But before he could complete his plan, one of the proposed astronomers, who had not yet received the letter of invitation, found a planetary object in the gap in question. He was Father Giuseppe Piazzi of Palermo, who, on January 1, 1801, spotted through his telescope a tiny, slowly moving point of light in the constellation of the Bull. He named it Ceres—a goddess sacred to his native Sicily and companion of Jupiter.

However, while observing the new planet on March 28, 1802, the German astronomer Heinrich Olbers discovered another small object in the Mars-Jupiter gap not far from Ceres. It was named Pallas (a daughter of Jupiter). In June 1802, Olbers wrote to Bode: "Did Ceres and Pallas always travel in their current orbits in peaceful proximity or are both part of the debris of a former and larger planet which exploded in a major catastrophe?" As it happens, it is estimated that there is not enough material between Mars and Jupiter to have comprised a planet, but astronomers today still consider that some violent events must have taken place there—perhaps between bodies smaller than planets which had their original orbits in this area.

Whatever the answer, more "asteroids" or "minor planets" were discovered—Juno in 1804 and Vesta in 1807 being the next ones. After a pause of 38 years, the fifth, Astraea, was found, and today there are more than 5000 asteroids with reliably-known orbits. Vesta is the only asteroid which is visible to the naked eye, this being just possible at favorable (though infrequent) oppositions. It orbits the Sun in 3.6 years, and oppositions occur about every 16.6 months. Vesta is estimated to have a diameter of between 500 and 600 kilometers.

Such is the story connected with the Titius-Bode Law. But when the planets Neptune and Pluto were discovered beyond Uranus, it was found that the law no longer held. Neptune was discovered in 1846, Pluto in 1930, both being much closer than the Titius-Bode Law predicted. If it is a genuine law of some kind, the two outer planets may be strangers to the rest of the planetary system. The table below compares the law's predictions with the planetary distances.

PLANET	MEAN DISTANCE IN A.U.	TITIUS-BODE LAW
Mercury	.39	.4
Venus	.72	.7
Earth	1.00	1.0
Mars	1.52	1.6
Ceres	2.77	2.8
Jupiter	5.20	5.2
Saturn	9.54	10.0
Uranus	19.18	19.6
Neptune	30.06	38.8
Pluto	39.44	77.2

TABLE 2

Another aspect of this table is that Pluto appears to fit with the law's next planetary position after Uranus, leaving Neptune as the only planet outside the prediction. It should be added that other, more sophisticated mathematical schemes have been devised this century, into which the orbits of all the known planets can be seen to fit in their correct order. (See *The Titius-Bode Law of Planetary Distances: Its History and Theory*, by Michael Nieto; Pergamon Press, 1972.)

B. The Platonic Solids

For interest I here add some details on Kepler's association of the five Platonic solids with the orbits of the planets, as mentioned in this chapter. Table 3 is derived from Chapter 21 of Kepler's *Mysterium Cosmographicum* (translated as *The Secret of the Universe* by A.M. Duncan; Abaris Books, New York, 1981. See also that book's introduction).

9.16	Saturn
9.16	Cube's circumsphere
5.26	Cube's insphere
5.25	Jupiter
1.65	Tetrahedron's insphere
1.52	Mars
1.10	Dodecahedron's insphere
1.00	Earth
.76	Icosahedron's insphere
.72	Venus
.43	Octahedron's insphere
.36	Mercury

TABLE 3

The numbers beside the planets in Table 3 are their mean distances from the Sun (based on Copernican, not modern calculations) expressed in astronomical units—as is the number for the radius of the circumsphere of the cube (the sphere which passes through its corners) and the numbers for the insphere (the sphere inside a Platonic solid which touches its faces).

The planets have maximum and minimum as well as mean distances, and the area between the maximum and minimum has to be pictured as the thickness of a shell or orb with the Sun as center. The spheres connected with the Platonic solids then lie on, within, or close to the surfaces of the corresponding planetary orbs.

In some calculations for the distance of Mercury, Kepler devised, as an alternative to the insphere of the octahedron, its midsphere or inside sphere touching its edges. Also, in a later work (*Harmonices Mundi*, Chapter 5) Kepler placed a solid of his own invention which he called a hedgehog (*echinus*) between the orbs of Mars and Venus. (Today this figure is called a small stellated dodecahedron. It is one of four modern solids which are regular but concave. The five Platonic solids are defined as convex.) When Kepler placed the twelve exterior points of the small stellated dodecahedron on the orb of Mars, the solid's twelve interior planes touched the orb of Venus.

The closeness of the Copernican-based planetary distances to the spheres of the solids in Table 3 shows how much Kepler's work supported the theory of Copernicus and confirmed it for people in his day. As a general picture, the scheme of Platonic solids from Saturn to Mercury is surprisingly apt, and even stands some comparison with modern values of the planetary distances.

Kepler's first words in the "Preface to the Reader" in *Mysterium Cosmographicum* are:

> It is my intention, reader, to show in this little book that the most great and good Creator, in the creation of this moving universe, and the arrangement of the heavens, looked to those five regular solids, which have been so celebrated from the time of Pythagoras and Plato down to our own, and that he fitted to the nature of those solids,

the number of the heavens, their proportions, and the law of their motions.

Modern writers usually dismiss Kepler's Platonic solids scheme in relation to the planets as fanciful and inaccurate. Yet J.V. Field in his *Kepler's Geometrical Cosmology* (University of Chicago Press, 1988, Chapter 3) reassesses the evidence and states: "...the fit between the calculated ratios for the Platonic solids and the observational ratios for the planetary orbs is very good. Until quite recently, twentieth-century cosmologists would have been very pleased if their theories had fitted the observations as well as Kepler's do." In notes to the same chapter, he adds that scepticism about this geometrical theory "has had the unfortunate effect of giving currency to the assumption that the theory is, at best, only in rough agreement with observation (and is thus different in spirit from Kepler's astronomical theories)."

One reason for the dismissal of the Platonic solids planetary scheme could be that, as quoted above, through it the "Creator" is said to determine "the number of the heavens"—i.e., six planets only—whereas since then the asteroids, Uranus, Neptune, and Pluto have been added. These last four are essentially invisible to the naked eye (Uranus and Vesta lie just at the limit of naked-eye visibility, but are below it most of the time), yet their laws of movement correspond to those found by Kepler for the other planets in his later works (e.g., the famous Three Laws of Kepler). So we have one overall set of mathematical laws for all the planets, and another visual, geometrical one for the regular naked-eye planets.

Chapter Eight

Comets and Meteors

Having considered the Sun as a center, and the movement of the planets in ellipses, we can now better study comets and meteors, since their appearances are found to relate so directly to conic curves (ellipses, parabolas, hyperbolas) and to a central role for the Sun.

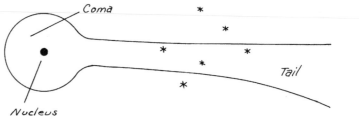

Figure 149

Many comets have three parts, as shown in Figure 149. The *nucleus* is surrounded by a fuzzy *coma* (both making up the head of the comet). The *tail* often has two aspects, the curved part being reflected sunlight (as is the nucleus) and the straight part being self-luminous. The coma is both luminous and reflective. Some comets do not develop a visible tail or nucleus, only a coma. The tail has a filmy, transparent appearance and, as in Figure 149, the stars can be seen easily through it.

The movements and appearances of comets have, in the past, been more of a mystery to geometrical thinking than even stars and planets. They are liable to appear in any part of the sky and, often with transparent tails streaming before or after them, march slowly and majestically in front of the stars from night to night over a period of weeks or months. They incline to defy prediction; the 6th-century A.D. Indian astronomer Varahamihira said that the appearances and paths of comets could not be discovered by mathematical calculations (such calculations not being developed until later centuries.) Even the great

Tycho Brahe said that comets were a wonderwork of God, coming from a hidden natural cause. At their first appearance, at least, comets surprise us with their unexpected presence and are like cosmic visitors, strangers among the familiar stars and planets. The early Chinese called them Broom Stars—visitors, perhaps, with a job to do. One comet was described by the ancient Chinese as a new broom sweeping away old traditions.

The Greeks of two thousand years ago saw comets as fiery emanations in the earth's atmosphere, originally arising as dry, dense exhalations from the Earth itself. Meteors were understood by them to be atmospheric phenomena also, and hence the connection with the word "meteorology"—the science of the atmosphere and weather.

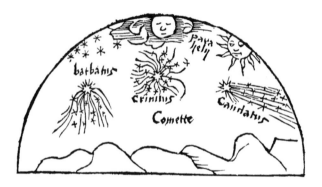

PLATE 12
Woodcut depicting comets in a 1512 edition of Aristotle's *Meteorologia*.
From *Watchers of the Stars*, by Patrick Moore; Michael Joseph Publishers, 1974.

Plate 12 is a 16th-century impression of "meteorological" activity from an edition of Aristotle's book *Meteorologia*. Comets certainly look as if they could be atmospheric phenomena, hanging like ghostly veils in front of the stars from night to night. But they are very much further away than the Earth's atmosphere, moving among the planets themselves, as was proved by Tycho Brahe when he observed the comet of 1577. He first saw this comet in the early evening of November 13 while fishing in a pond at his observatory on the Danish island of Hveen. It then appeared to him as a brilliant star, already visible just before sunset. After sunset he saw that it was a comet with its head in the stars of the Archer and a magnificent curved tail extending 22 degrees (from thumb to little finger on a hand spread out at arm's length) into the constellation of the Goat. He saw that the head was white light and the tail, somewhat bent in the middle, was of a burning, dark red color, like a flame penetrating through smoke. The comet was to remain visible for more than two months, its head moving in that time across a quarter of the sky from near the ecliptic up into Pegasus.

Many astronomers in different parts of the world observed this comet as well, but Tycho Brahe's observations and calculations of its positions and movements were the most accurate. He determined that the comet was much further from the Earth than the Moon, using a method called diurnal parallax. In Figure 150 the Earth is considered motionless, and a star appears to move during the night from overhead down toward the western horizon. Because it is the rotation of the Earth on its axis which causes this movement, the center of the star's apparent motion is the center of the Earth. This also applies to the nightly motion of other objects in the sky, for example the much closer Moon. While the apparent nightly movement of the Moon has the center of its motion at the center of the Earth, the observer at A in Figure 150 is on the surface of the Earth, not at its center, and if star and Moon are in line when in the south, then they will not appear so when setting; the closer Moon will appear shifted downward in relation to the star (broken line in the figure). The amount of shift has to take into account the Moon's own motion against the stars during this time, but this is easily subtracted from the observed positions.

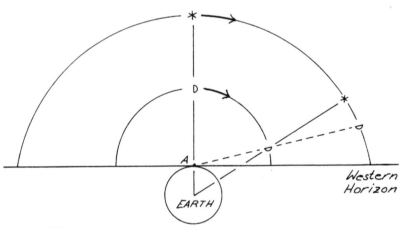

Figure 150

This is a simplified representation of diurnal parallax, but using this principle with the star designated Epsilon [ε] in Pegasus, Tycho Brahe found through careful measurement that the comet of 1577 had a diurnal parallax shift at least substantially smaller than the Moon's. In fact, it was so small that it could not be determined accurately. This meant that the comet must be beyond the Moon. After further considerations and calculations, Brahe assumed the comet to be almost the distance of Venus (just outside the orbit of Venus and circling round the Sun).

Modern calculations indicate that this comet of 1577 passed closer to the Sun than Brahe thought—in fact to within the orbit of Mercury. Before and after that it travelled on, or almost on, the path of a parabola, which means that it is not expected to return. Nevertheless, Tycho Brahe's contribution to the modern understanding of cometary motions was great, and he achieved much in establishing that they lie beyond the Earth's atmosphere and move round the Sun.

Comets are understood to originate beyond the planetary system and only enter it when drawn by the attraction of the Sun. Their paths, by nature, are parabolas, so that ideally an individual comet makes a once-only appearance, never returning. This is because a parabola is a conic curve with one of its points geometrically at infinity. But the paths of comets are also influenced by the attraction of the planets, and are often diverted into ellipses and hyperbolas. A comet travelling on a hyperbola would not return either. Figure 151 shows these three types of curve, which the student can construct as explained in the exercise at the end of this chapter.

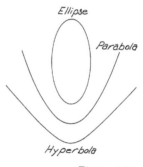

Figure 151

Comets which move round the Sun in ellipses have really become members of the planetary system. The comet with the shortest-known period of return is Encke's which moves round the Sun, from inside the orbit of Mercury to the asteroid belt within the orbit of Jupiter, in only 3.3 years. It is mostly not visible to the naked eye and was first seen in January 1786 through the telescope of Pierre Mechain when the comet was in the constellation of the Waterman. But the comet now takes its name from Johann Encke who realized it was a periodic comet and correctly predicted its return for 1822 and 1825.

The most famous prediction of a comet's return is the first one—successfully made by the English astronomer Edmond Halley. He calculated that a comet seen in August 1682 would return in 1758. Halley died in 1742, but on Christmas night, 1758, a German amateur astronomer Johann Palitzch sighted the return of the comet, which is now the famed Halley's Comet, returning approximately every 76 years. Its next visit will be in the summer skies of 2061.

Halley's prediction was certainly the first for Europe, but it seems that in India there was a belief in the periodicity of comets before that. The 6th-century A.D. astronomer Bhadrabahu writes, "...the maximum period of [the] disappearance of a comet is 36 years; the average period, 27 years; and the minimum period, 13 years." Later, the 10th-century astronomer Bhattotpala listed comets with return periods ranging from 100 to 1500 years. How these periods were arrived at is not known, though on the evidence of the earlier-mentioned astronomer Varahamihira, it was presumably not with mathematical calculations like Halley's.

PLATE 13

Halley's Comet of 1531 in the constellation of the Lion, depicted in *Practica*, by Peter Apian, in the same year.

From *Fire and Ice*, by Roberta Olson; Walker and Company, New York, 1985.

However, it was by pure observation that the early Chinese first discovered that the tails of comets always point away from the Sun. This direction of the tail was first realized among Europeans by Peter Apian (Petrus Apianus) in Germany, and the idea is clearly portrayed in his book illustration of Halley's Comet in 1531 as it passed above the Sun in the constellation of the Lion (Plate 13). A comet becomes visible only when it nears the Sun, because it is only then that it can grow a coma and tail, and that the nucleus can brighten. It also moves swiftest in its orbit when nearest to the Sun (the focus of its orbit), then slows down and fades into obscurity for years or eons, or forever.

Figure 152 shows, diagrammatically, the progress of Halley's Comet from its closest approach to the Sun (perihelion), to beyond the orbit of Neptune (aphelion) and back, over the next decades. Figure 153 shows how the path of Halley's Comet passes between the orbits of Mercury and Venus and displays its tail shortly before, during, and after that. On its return in 1985/86, the tiny nucleus and coma were first visible to the naked eye only as a dim patch of light in the constellation of the Bull in November 1985, when the comet had already almost reached the orbit of Mars. Perihelion was reached on February 9, 1986.

Because comets move round the Sun in their conic curves, they scatter behind them a trail of particles, from dust, to pebble-sized objects, to larger pieces of material. The path of the Earth through space frequently crosses one or other of the

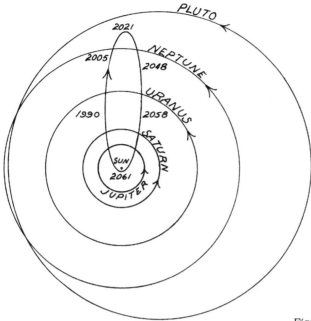

Figure 152

cometary orbits with its scattering of particles, though many
cometary orbits are missed altogether by the Earth since
objects in space all have different orbital planes. The main
point is whether the Earth in its orbit crosses the comet's
orbit, from whatever angle, in three-dimensional space.
When this happens the Earth's atmosphere strikes against
the scattered particles, and, even if the particles are only the
size of grains of sand, we see meteors flashing across the
nighttime sky. This is understood to be the cause of most
meteors or (in popular language) shooting stars.

Figure 153

In the case of Comet Halley, the meteors thought to be connected with its orbit occur in the Waterman (Eta Aquarids
shower) in May and in Orion (Orionids shower) in October.
This does not necessarily mean that the meteor flashes pass
across these constellations, but rather that a small area
within each of them is the origin of the flashes which then
become visible often far from the constellation itself. The
place of origin is called the radiant, and seen from Earth the
meteors appear, because of perspective, to radiate round the
sky from this source. Just as railway tracks appear, by perspective, to be converging toward a point, so meteors appear
to radiate in all directions from one small area, but in space
are moving parallel to each other.

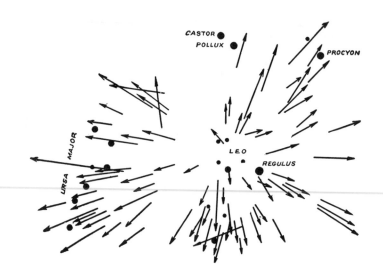

Plate 14 is a drawing of Leonid meteor trails made on a November night at Brown University in Rhode Island. Here the perspective effect can be seen, with three or four exceptions from other sources. But the student must not be led into thinking that such a sight will normally meet the eye on observing the Leonids. The trails in Plate 14 were recorded over a period of 5 hours. Usually we see one isolated, silent streak lasting no more than a second. To the naked eye, meteors are mostly elusive borderline phenomena, which flash for a moment without warning into our range of vision and keep us waiting, often for many minutes, until the next one appears. Yet the term used to describe this is a "shower" of meteors, which is misleading for the beginner. Very rarely do meteors "rain" across the skies; the Leonids just mentioned normally have a maximum of about 10 to 15 meteors an hour around November 17—and this only in the ideal situation of the radiant being overhead and in a clear, dark sky.

Despite this, the Leonid shower has, from time to time, provided exceptional displays in which meteors have splashed across the sky like a snowstorm in heaven. The Leonids were responsible for what is considered the greatest meteor display ever recorded, when, on a November morning in 1966, an estimate of over 2000 meteors a minute brought the sky alive. The Leonids are associated with Comet Tempel-Tuttle which has a return period of 33 years, and increased activity of the shower has taken place in multiples of 33 years. Astronomers are hoping for another spectacular display on November 18, 1999.

Shortly before dawn when the sky is still dark is the optimum time for meteors. The reason for this is illustrated in Figure 154 which shows the Earth rotating anticlockwise through its shadow and also moving through space (in orbit round the Sun) toward the right. This orbital direction (identified by a point on the ecliptic for the Earth observer) is high overhead at dawn for someone near the Earth's equator. Further into the Northern Hemisphere this direction is above the horizon toward the south. Therefore the leading side of the Earth's atmosphere, which encounters meteoric material in space, is above the horizon for the predawn observer and more meteors can be seen if the radiant is also above the horizon. This situation occurs for the Perseid shower, the radiant of which is well above the horizon and rising from midnight to dawn on the date of its peak, around August 12. It is the best known of all regular showers and was observed as long ago as A.D. 36 by the Chinese, who wrote on that occasion that "more than 100 meteors flew thither in the morning." It is also the most popular shower since it occurs on summer nights; the best way to observe it is to lie outside on one's back on a campbed from midnight on (into the morning of, for example, August 12) to give as wide a view as possible of the sky dome. One can expect an average of around one meteor a minute.

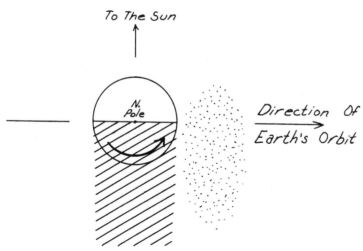

Figure 154

Before summer vacation, students can be told to watch out for the Perseids (radiating from the constellation of Perseus, that is). But during or close to term time, probably the best showers to note are the Orionids (maximum activity around October 21), the Geminids (maximum around December 13) and the Quadrantids (radiant in the constellation of Boötes, maximum around January 3). All the above showers should be looked for particularly in the early morning hours of the day of maximum. One factor which can interfere with viewing, however, is the Moon, which lightens the sky if it is in the vicinity at the time.

The meteor streaks (or trails) one normally sees have their origin in tiny grains of matter that burn up and vaporize on coming into contact with the Earth's atmosphere. But larger pieces of material also enter the atmosphere from time to time, and these can cause brilliant, colored, and prolonged streaks of light brighter than the planet Venus. These are called fireballs. They can happen at any time and are not necessarily associated with meteor showers. But when they occur, there are likely to be falls of *meteorites* (not meteors, which are flashes of light) onto the ground. Meteorites can vary from tons in weight to an ounce or less, and are classified into irons, stony-irons, and stones. Their origin is essentially a mystery, though many scientists think that they may come from the asteroid belt, the ring of small planetary objects scattered mostly between the orbits of Mars and Jupiter. It has been estimated that around 19,000 meteorites with masses of at least 4 ounces fall on the globe of the earth each year, about 5,800 of them falling on land and the rest falling in the sea. Natural history and geological museums usually have a meteorite section for students to visit, and it is always worthwhile for a school to purchase some pieces of meteorite for students to study and handle in the classroom.

With the descent of "stones from the sky" down onto the Earth, we can conclude our theme so far and bring the subject back down to where it started—at the spot where the observer stands, gazing upward into the starry vault and fixing positions in space in relation to where he or she is. It remains to add something about what the sky looks like from the Southern Hemisphere, then to provide some astronomical material from poetry for possible classroom use.

Supplementary Exercises

1.

The following drawings show constructions for the three conic curves that comets can trace, using an "equal distances" method. Points on the curve are equidistant from a focus and points on a circle (in the case of the ellipse and hyperbola) or points on a straight line (parabola).

The ellipse is formed if a focus to the curve is placed inside the circle (Figure 155), and the hyperbola if a focus is placed outside (Figure 156).

In Figure 155 concentric equidistant circles are first drawn (center A) and a focus (B) chosen on the circle next to the outermost. This outermost circle we can call the "base" circle. Circles are then drawn, with B as center, touching the other circles. Point C, for example, is the intersection of the third circle from B with the third circle from the base. The lines BC and CD (the latter passing through A) are equal, and C is a point on the ellipse. It is then found, on completing the construction, that A is the other focus.

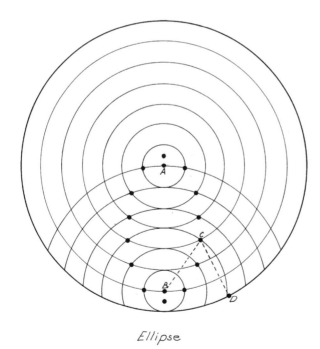

Ellipse

Figure 155

Figure 156 uses exactly the same construction as Figure 155, but starts with focus B outside the "base" circle DF. The lines BC and CD are equal again (also BE and EF).

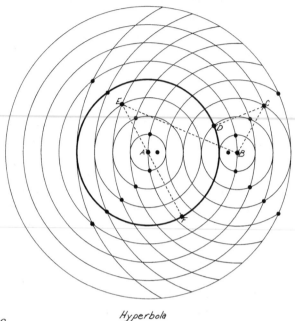

Figure 156   *Hyperbola*

Figure 157 can be started with the bottom "base" line (part of a circle with infinite radius). Point B is chosen, say, one centimeter perpendicularly above it and a circle drawn with center B and radius one centimeter; then a circle with radius two centimeters, and others concentric and equidistant. Lines parallel to the base line are drawn tangent to the circles. The parallel lines again represent parts of circles with infinite radii. This time CD is drawn at right angles to the base line and passes through the other focus (A) at infinity.

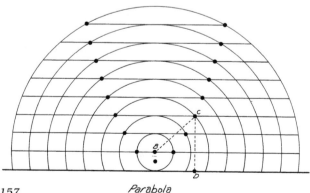

Figure 157   *Parabola*

2.

Here we can connect the movements of comets with a geometrical theorem and, working in a plane, establish that comets move in conic curves.

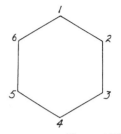

Figure 158 is a hexagon with its points numbered clockwise from 1 to 6. One can see that side 1,2 is opposite to side 4,5; side 2,3 opposite to 5,6; and side 3,4 opposite to 6,1.

Figure 158

Figure 159 is also a hexagon (though irregular) with its points on a conic curve (a circle in this case). The Theorem of Pascal states that the lines which form opposite sides of a hexagon (however drawn) on a conic curve intersect on a straight line (Figure 160).

Figure 159

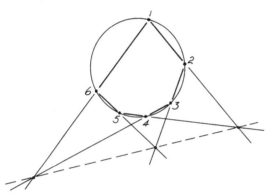

Figure 160

A projective geometrical proof of this involves the fact that the intersections of corresponding projective lines through two points lie on a conic curve. Details of a proof can be worked out in high school classes and can readily be found in books on synthetic projective geometry.

Figure 161 shows six possible plots of a comet's position represented in a plane. Figure 162 establishes that these same positions are on a conic curve (in this case a parabola), since opposite sides of the hexagon intersect on a straight line.

Figure 161

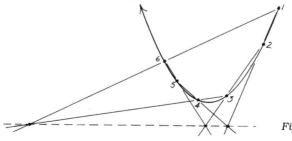

Figure 162

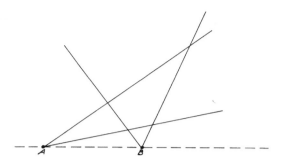

Figure 163

This theorem was called the Mystic Hexagram by its discoverer Blaise Pascal (1623-1662). It has many valuable properties and is one of the most fruitful laws of geometry to be found since the Greeks. No less remarkable is the fact that Pascal discovered it when he was only 16 years of age.

If one does not have a template for a conic curve to make such drawings as in the previous two figures, then by reversing the principle one can plot six points on a possible cometary orbit. Start with the broken line and choose any two points A and B on it. Draw two lines from each point so that a quadrilateral is formed inside them (Figure 163).

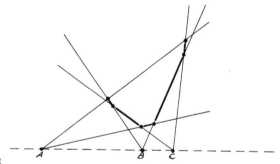

Figure 164

Choose a third point C on the broken line and cut off two corners of the quadrilateral (Figure 164). Instead of a quadrilateral, we now have a hexagon inside the lines. The six corners lie on a conic curve and can be positions of a comet. However, with this construction the curve could be an ellipse, hyperbola, or parabola though a comet's orbit could be any of these three.

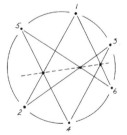

Figure 165

Figure 165 shows how opposite sides of a six-sided figure with its corners on a conic curve intersect on a straight line, whatever the shape of the figure (i.e., in whatever way the six points are connected by six lines).

Chapter Nine

The Southern Hemisphere Sky

With deference to those students dwelling in the Southern Hemisphere, I regret not having written this book from their perspective from the start, but that is another task. I am a Northern Hemisphere dweller and, by nature, picture the sky from there; but for this text at least, an outline of sky appearances from the other side of the world is very necessary for the education of students in the north. For Southern Hemisphere readers, a translation of basic sky views into a Southern perspective will help to make more sense of the earlier chapters.

If one has studied the sky intently from the Northern Hemisphere and made it part of oneself, it is a matter of astonishment to travel south of the equator and experience, for the first time, the sky turning the other way round—even when one is prepared for it. The sky and its movements are part of the natural environment and if one lives consciously with nature, it is a special and moving occasion to experience directly a completely different "greater environment" of circling stars.

Perhaps, then, one can understand the Greek historian Herodotus, who lived around 450 B.C., saying in Book 4 of his *History* that it did "not seem credible" that the Sun should rise on the opposite side of the sky in the Southern Hemisphere. He tells the story of how the Egyptian king Neco had wanted to show that Africa was surrounded by water in the south. In those days the upper part of Africa was as far south as the peoples of the Mediterranean had ventured. King Neco dispatched some Phoenicians, whose people lived on the coast of Syria and were famous for their skills in seafaring, from the northern end of the Red Sea with orders to sail south and then clockwise round Africa, returning to the Mediterranean and Egypt through the Pillars of Hercules

(Straits of Gibraltar). The voyage took over two years, and when the ships returned the sailors reported that while sailing round the southern part of Africa they had the Sun on their "right hand." This means that as they faced that part of the sky which the zodiac generally spans and where Sun, Moon, and planets are visible, the Sun rose on their right. This kind of scene Coleridge describes when the ship in "The Rime of the Ancient Mariner" is blown into the South Seas by a storm:

> The Sun now rose upon the right:
> Out of the sea came he,
> Still hid in mist, and on the left
> Went down into the sea.

This Herodotus found difficult to believe. A glance at Figure 44 shows the Sun rising on the left as one faces the direction of its daytime arc. However, Herodotus did add that though the sailors' story did not seem credible to him, it may be credible to others. Let us take him up on this. The best demonstration is again the trusty celestial globe.

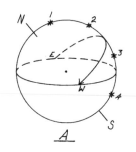

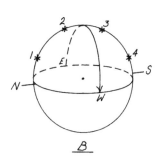

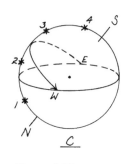

Figure 166

Figure 166 shows three positions of the celestial sphere representing the view from three different latitudes on Earth. The sphere at position A is the one we were hitherto familiar with, for example in Figure 3 of this book, for the Northern Hemisphere. The curved line is the celestial equator, with the arrow indicating the direction of rotation of the sphere (east to west), in which direction the Sun also moves in a day. The numbers 1, 2, 3, 4 denote four stars on the sphere. In sphere position A, with the observer at the center, when the observer looks toward the celestial equator, star 2 is above star 3. Star 4 is invisible below the horizon, as is the south celestial pole.

Sphere position B shows the sky for the observer at the Earth's equator. Here, stars 2 and 3 are equally high overhead, but star 4 is now visible. The north and south celestial poles both lie on the horizon.

Sphere position C has turned the globe even further, so that the north celestial pole is now below the horizon, while the south celestial pole has risen above it and the observer sees a Southern Hemisphere sky. Now star 1 is invisible. But the observer in the center who faces the celestial equator sees the star 3 *above* star 2—the opposite to what was observed in sphere position A in the Northern Hemisphere. Also, we can now understand what the Phoenician sailors experienced. Facing toward the celestial equator, the Sun would rise on their right-hand side, not on their left as in sphere position A. Yet it can be seen that the Sun would still be rising in the east on all three spheres. Going south of the equator, the sky turns the other way round, but the names of the compass directions remain the same.

On their voyage, the Phoenician sailors landed at certain points on the southern African coast to sow crops with seed they carried on board, then harvested them for food before sailing on. During this time they had plenty of opportunity to study the familiar stars from a different angle and learn new constellations and star movements as well. What they saw in general holds good for other places south of the equator, such as Australia, New Zealand, and South America.

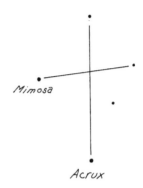

Figure 167

From the southern end of Africa looking south at night, they would see the stars rotate *clockwise* round the south celestial pole. One group of four stars (with a fainter fifth) which they would have seen moving round the pole is today part of the constellation Crux or, commonly, the Southern Cross (Figure 167). In Greek times these stars were within a constellation called the Centaur, but in the fifteenth or sixteenth century they were separated off into a small constellation of their own, which is the smallest constellation on the whole celestial sphere. Figure 168 shows the movement of the Southern Cross in 6-hour intervals over 24 hours. The Cross is about 4-1/2 times its length from the south celestial pole, and its long axis points just to the left of the pole when the Cross is near the horizon. The Cross stands within the Milky Way, and inside its orbit round the pole are the circumpolar stars of the Southern Hemisphere, viewed at around 35 degrees south latitude.

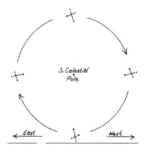

Figure 168

The five main stars of the Southern Cross can be made out at the top of the circle and surrounding the letter B in Plate 15. This fanciful drawing was done in 1517 by the Italian navigator Andrea Corsali, who wrote, "This crosse is so fayre and beutiful, that none other hevenly sygne may be compared to it as may appear by this fygure." The Portuguese naturalist Cristoval d'Acosta called the five stars the Southern Celestial Clock, and reading the time by them is aided by the fact that the axis of the cross points toward the center of its orbital circle and moves like an hour hand. Alexander von Humboldt, in his *Voyage to the Equinoctial Regions of the New Continent* (South America) confirms that there were many peoples in the Southern Hemisphere who told the time by these stars, though he also says of the Portuguese and Spaniards that "A religious sentiment attaches them to a constellation the form of which recalls the sign of the faith planted by their ancestors in the deserts of the New World." In 1508 a map printed in Rome labelled South America as the Land of the Holy Cross. Meanwhile, the Peruvians called the stars of the Cross a heavenly Doe suckling its fawn.

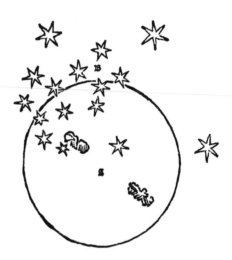

The aforementioned Andrea Corsali believed that the famous Italian poet Dante (1265-1321) had prophesied the existence of the Southern Cross in his visionary poem *Purgatory*. Dante describes Purgatory as an island mountain in the Southern Hemisphere, at the top of which is Eden or Paradise. When Dante and his companion, Virgil, arrive at the island, having passed through the center of the Earth, they see four bright stars near the south celestial pole. Were they the stars of the Southern Cross? Scholars today incline to doubt it (the stars don't seem to be in the right position for the time of night, date, and presumed latitude described in the poem) or else feel that Dante heard about these stars from contemporary travellers. Those who do claim that Dante was referring to the Southern Cross include Alexander von Humboldt and the poet Longfellow, the latter translating Dante's relevant lines in *Purgatory* as:

...and fixed my mind
Upon the other pole and saw four stars
N'er seen before save by the primal people

Dante also calls the northern parts a

...widowed site
Because thou art deprived of seeing these!

—"these" being his four Southern stars.

"Widowed" is an apt term, for the fact is that because of a gradual shift in the relation of the star sphere to the celestial equator (precession of the equinoxes) over many centuries, the stars of the Southern Cross were above the horizon 5000 years ago as far north as the latitude of London, England. Since then their limit of visibility has crept south to about the latitude of Miami in Florida. Richard Allen in his book *Star Names: Their Lore and Meaning* says that the Southern Cross "was last seen on the horizon of Jerusalem...about the time that Christ was crucified"—take that as one may.

Gazing at the actual stars of the Cross from the Southern Hemisphere once more, one notices beside it a dark patch of sky with no stars (Figure 169). Astronomers today identify this as a "dark nebula" or cloud of gas and dust which obscures many stars behind it. It is called the Coal Sack. It was first formally described by the Italian historian Peter Martyr (1455-1526), and it has also been named Magellan's Spot. The English historian James Froude (1818-1894) called it "the inky spot—an opening into the awful solitude of unoccupied space." An Australian Aboriginal legend describes it as "the embodiment of evil in the shape of an emu, who lies in wait at the foot of a tree, represented by the stars of the Cross, for an opossum driven by his persecutions to take refuge among its branches."

Figure 169

The Coal Sack is one way of identifying the Southern Cross with certainty, for there are two other similar-looking asterisms in the sky which could be confused with it—the stars popularly known as the False Cross, and the Diamond Cross. These are shown in Figure 170 which depicts the southern view between 10 and 11 p.m. in the middle of January.

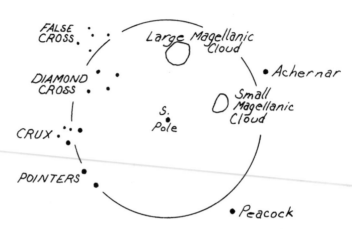

Figure 170

The False Cross and the Diamond Cross are fainter than the main stars of the Southern Cross and originally were part of a constellation called Argo, which mythologies connected with the ship Argo that carried Jason and the Argonauts on their voyage to recover the Golden Fleece. Alternatively, the Greek astronomer Eratosthenes (who lived around 250 B.C.) said that the constellation represented the first ship to sail the ocean before Jason's time, while an Egyptian story describes it as the ark in which Isis and Osiris escaped the Flood. Argo has been obsolete since last century when it was divided up into the constellations Carina, Puppis, Vela, and Pyxis.

The brightest star in Argo was Canopus, which now stands in Carina. It is the second brightest star in the sky, second only to Sirius. Its name was apparently given to it by Eratosthenes. During the course of time it has been called the star of Osiris; the Hindus called it Agastya, one of the wise teachers (rishis); and in China it was worshipped as Laou Jin, the Old Man.

Between Canopus and the south celestial pole is the Large Magellanic Cloud, a ghostly patch of dim light, with the Small Magellanic Cloud nearby. Modern astronomers have identified these as two small galaxies which are close neighbors of our own galaxy. They are named after the Portuguese navigator Ferdinand Magellan, who recorded them in 1519, though they were also known as the Cape Clouds by early seafarers rounding the Cape of Good Hope. The Italian explorer Marco Polo

(1254-1324) seemed to be describing the Large Magellanic Cloud when he reported how he saw a marvellous star as big as a sack. He certainly had travelled far enough south, for he says elsewhere that he had seen the south celestial pole "a spear's length" above the horizon.

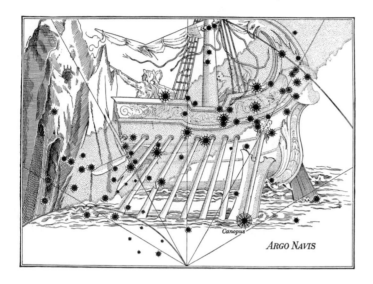

ARGO NAVIS

PLATE 16
The now-obsolete constellation of Argo Navis, after a drawing by the German astronomer Johann Bayer in his 1603 star atlas, *Uranometria.*

The Small Magellanic Cloud is between the south celestial pole and a conspicuous star called Achernar in the constellation Eridanus (the river), the largest constellation in the sky, meandering from Achernar to beside Rigel in Orion. Eratosthenes considered it to be the heavenly counterpart of the Nile which flows, like Eridanus, from south to north. It has also been called by the Greeks, including the astronomer Hipparchus (c. 150 B.C.), the River of Orion. The name Achernar is from the Arabic meaning the End of the River.

Further round the southern end of the celestial sphere (Figure 170) is the fainter Peacock star (Alpha Pavonis), the brightest star in the constellation from which it takes its name—Pavo, the Peacock. This name was given to the constellation by the German astronomer Johann Bayer in the seventeenth century. Legend says that Argos, the builder of the ship Argo, was changed into a peacock by the goddess Juno.

Remaining on the map in Figure 170 are two stars called the Pointers, and they bring us back full circle to the constellation of the Centaur. These two stars are at the forefeet of the mythical Centaur—half man, half horse. Although the

Southern Cross was separated off from this constellation, the Pointers still remain within it and point to the Cross itself, a sure aid to identification of the true Crux. The Bushmen of South Africa called the Pointers the Two Men that once were Lions, and the Australian Aboriginals said they were Two Brothers who killed Tchingal with their spears.

The furthest of the two Pointer stars from the Cross is Alpha Centauri, the third brightest star in the sky. Another name for it is Rigil (Rigel) Kentauris, from the Arabic for Centaur's Foot, just as another star Rigel is at the foot of Orion. Today Alpha Centauri is the more famous of the Pointers because in 1839 it was discovered to be the nearest star system to our Sun. One says "star system" for it was found to be a double star in 1689 by a Father Richaud during telescopic observations in India. It has since been determined that one star orbits round the other in about 80 years. Then in 1915 a much smaller star was discovered, seemingly connected to the other two, which made this a triple star system. The third star is called Proxima (meaning "nearest") Centauri because it is judged to be slightly nearer to us than the other two. Seen from the Alpha Centauri group, our Sun would look like a bright star shining between the constellations of Perseus and Cassiopeia, but the Earth and its planets would be too small and close to the Sun to be visible, even with a telescope.

The other star of the Pointers, between Alpha Centauri and the Cross, is called Hadar, taken from an Arabic proper name. Ptolemy described this star as being situated on the knee of the Centaur's left front leg.

As can be seen, the stars near the south celestial pole are rich in interest and historical background, and at least some of it should be common knowledge north and south of the equator. For the serious student there is much fascinating sky lore to be discovered if one looks for it.

The Zodiac and Celestial Equator

We can now take an overview of the rest of the sky seen from southern latitudes, this time in the directions of east, north, and west. The first thing which the observer familiar with northern latitudes discovers is that the stars are ones he or she knows already, only their patterns are inverted and they move the opposite way. For example, the figure of Orion, the center of which lies on the celestial equator, will appear with the star Rigel at the top left and will move from right to left as in Figure 171.

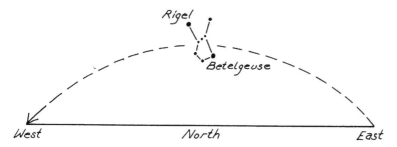

Figure 171

Figure 172 shows the stars plotted for midnight at the Southern Hemisphere midwinter (June). The view is for a geographical latitude of 50 degrees south (southern regions of Argentina and Chile). The reason for choosing such a southerly latitude is that an altitude (height of a star above the horizon) and azimuth (distance of it along the horizon) chart like this would have the zodiacal constellations disappear off the top for lower latitudes. The upper part of the zodiac would be more than 90 degrees altitude, or beyond overhead—stretching behind the observer facing north, thus not allowing all of the visible zodiac to be represented on one plane.

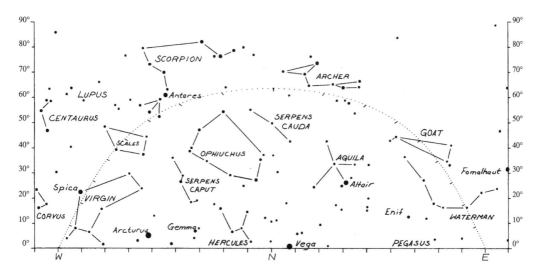

Figure 172

But a 50 degree south latitude chart can be representative for many southern latitudes and has the advantage of showing the midwinter zodiacal stars in one picture, without resorting to an additional overhead map. It gives a more visually whole impression while still orientating to a straight-line horizon. Another consideration is that for lower latitudes at midwinter midnight, the ecliptic itself would approach close to the overhead point and this would distort its curve toward becoming three sides of a rectangle.

Figure 173 shows the stars plotted for midnight in the Southern Hemisphere for midsummer (December). The view is for a geographical latitude of 35 degrees south (southern Australia, northern New Zealand, and southern South America).

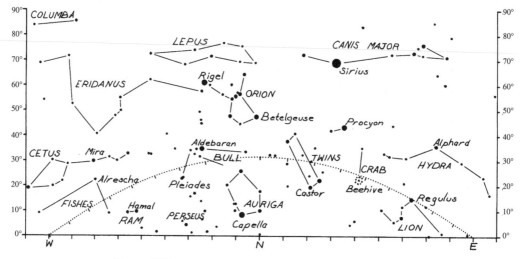

Figure 173

These two maps together provide a useful spread of stars for the Southern Hemisphere observer looking northward, at the same time allowing the stars to be pictured against a straight-line horizon and including the whole zodiac in two maps—as was done for the Northern Hemisphere in Chapter 2.

In order to draw such altitude/azimuth maps freehand for demonstration, it might be best to construct the curve of the celestial equator east to west for one's own latitude, using the method described at the end of Chapter 2. Then the ecliptic can be drawn freehand above the celestial equator for the midwinter midnight map, and below it for the midsummer midnight one; the zodiacal constellations' main stars can be taken from Figures 172 and 173, and those of some other constellations can be added.

It will be noticed that a seasonal reversal of the constellations has taken place compared with Figures 38 and 39. For example, at the northern midwinter midnight the constellations of the Twins and the Bull are high above the horizon, whereas at the southern midwinter midnight it is the Scorpion and Archer which stand high. The months are also opposite, midwinter being December in the Northern Hemisphere but June in the Southern. To understand this, one can take a celestial globe and place the Sun at, say, the solstice point in the zodiac between the Scorpion and the Archer. Then set the globe for the Northern Hemisphere at midnight, and the stars of the Twins and the Bull stand high above the horizon with the Sun far beneath it. It is midwinter. Keep the Sun where it is in the zodiac, so that it is still December, and move the *south* celestial pole above the horizon. Now you are in the Southern Hemisphere at midnight and the same stars of the Twins and the Bull now stand *low* above the horizon, with the Sun not far beneath it. It is midsummer, but still December.

Sun and Moon

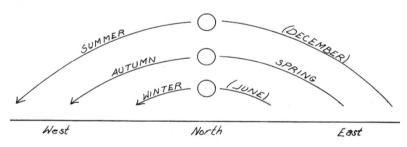

Figure 174

As with the stars, so must the appearances and movements of the Sun and Moon be reversed between the two hemispheres. Figure 174 shows the daily path of the Sun above the horizon for the four seasons in the Southern Hemisphere.

The first crescent Moon of the month will appear in the west in the evening, but with the crescent turned the other way from how it appears in the Northern Hemisphere (Figure 175).

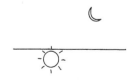

Figure 175

For someone accustomed to Northern Hemisphere experience it looks like a waning Moon, but in fact is a waxing one.

Figure 176 gives the phases and positions of the waxing Moon at sunset for the first half of the lunar month.

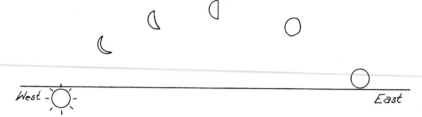

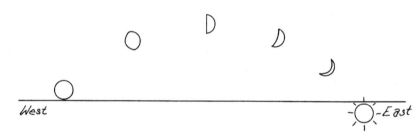

Figure 176

Figure 177 gives the phases and positions of the waning Moon at sunrise for the second half of the lunar month.

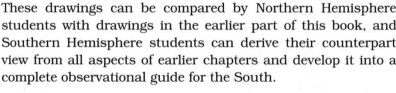

Figure 177

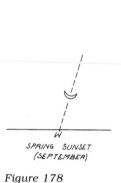

SPRING SUNSET
(SEPTEMBER)

Figure 178

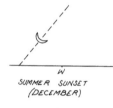

SUMMER SUNSET
(DECEMBER)

Figure 179

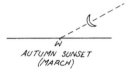

AUTUMN SUNSET
(MARCH)

Figure 180

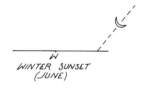

WINTER SUNSET
(JUNE)

Figure 181

The relationship of the ecliptic (and, therefore, of the zodiac, Moon, and planets) to the horizon at sunset during the four seasons is shown in Figures 178 to 181.

These drawings can be compared by Northern Hemisphere students with drawings in the earlier part of this book, and Southern Hemisphere students can derive their counterpart view from all aspects of earlier chapters and develop it into a complete observational guide for the South.

Supernova 1987A

It is appropriate that this part of the text ends with mention of an astronomical event of great interest to observers all over the world, which took place in the Southern Hemisphere.

Around midnight, or not long after, on the night of February 23/24, 1987, Oscar Duhalde, a Night Assistant at the remote mountain observatory of Las Campanas in Chile, took a coffee break and walked outside to look at the sky. It was a very clear night, and from his latitude of about 29 degrees south he could see the Large Magellanic Cloud well above the horizon. He also saw a fairly modest-looking star shining in the cloud— yet it was not the star's brightness which distinguished it at that moment, but its very presence. It changed the map of the sky, for where it shone no such star had shone before which was visible to the naked eye [marked * in Figure 182).

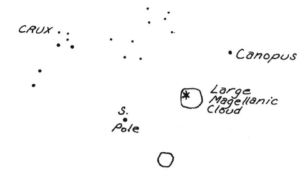

Figure 182

Oscar Duhalde was the first human who is known to have set eyes on the major New Star (supernova) event in the heavens for 383 years. Modern astronomy describes such an event as the explosion and disintegration of a star. In 1604, Kepler's Supernova lit up in the constellation of Ophiuchus. Kepler's star was in our galaxy, and not since then had another supernova been seen in, or neighboring, our galaxy until the night of February 23/24, 1987. This was the first supernova easily visible to the naked eye since the invention of the telescope. (It should be noted that supernovae are cataclysmic events happening only once, and must be distinguished from novae which are also stars that explode, but this does not result in their destruction and the event is liable to happen again. There have been a number of visible novae since 1604.)

As it happens, Oscar Duhalde did not report his momentous discovery to other astronomers at the observatory, but later that morning when they discussed it he told them that he had seen the star. He knew that part of the sky very well through his work and knew that the star had not been there before, but perhaps he did not quite realize the importance of it to science. However, around the time he looked up at this stranger which stood just south of the Tarantula Nebula (which is visible to the naked eye) in the Large Magellanic Cloud, a camera attached to a telescope in another nearby dome on the site had taken photographs of the same part of the sky. The telescope was being used by Ian Shelton, a young Canadian astronomer working on behalf of the University of Toronto. In the early hours of the morning of February 24, Ian Shelton developed the film before going to bed, and noticed that a star which had been very faint the night before had considerably brightened. He then walked outside to see it for himself. This time the star's importance dawned on the human mind. Shelton went over to speak to astronomers at the telescope where Oscar Duhalde was working and asked them what such an object would be that suddenly appeared in the Large Magellanic Cloud. The answer was that it must be a supernova, not just a nova.

Oscar Duhalde then said he had seen the star earlier with the naked eye. Everyone went outside under a bright, star-studded sky—mountain desert sites being chosen by astronomers because of the clarity and steadiness of seeing conditions. The new star was easily visible in the constellation of Dorado, the Swordfish (originally the Gold Fish), and was about 4 degrees from the pole of the ecliptic. It is now called Supernova 1987A, the letter A identifying it as the first supernova discovered in 1987. Other supernovae are often discovered, but not in our galaxy.

Later that morning a telegram officially announcing the discovery was sent to the International Astronomical Union in Cambridge, Massachusetts, and from there reached the front pages of the world's newspapers. Meanwhile the supernova slowly became more visible, at maximum in May 1987 being as bright as the star Algenib (Gamma Pegasi = +2.86 visual magnitude) one of the four stars of the "Square of Pegasus," or of about the same visual brightness as the fainter star of the four main stars of the Southern Cross (Delta Crucis = +2.81 visual magnitude). As the supernova brightened, it's color became redder before dimming to the threshold of naked-eye visibility by the end of the year.

This whole event brought worldwide attention not only to supernovae but to the astronomers and skies of the Southern

Hemisphere. It kindled a new general interest in the lore of the universe—and how many astronomy enthusiasts in the Northern Hemisphere knew, before 1987, that the south pole of the ecliptic was situated in the head, or eye, of the Swordfish?

As ordinary members of the public we may not see a supernova for the first time like Oscar Duhalde did. But let us hope that our teachers at school acquaint us sufficiently with our greater environment, the circling stars as they are seen with the naked eye, so that as adults our enthusiasm for the universe can be carried further, and so that we do not share Thomas Carlyle's lament quoted on a front page of this book.

Supplementary Exercises

1.
A demonstration of how geometrical symmetry works above and below the equator can be derived from how a particular constellation looks from the Northern and Southern Hemispheres. In Figure 183 five stars of the Twins are shown at the top as they appear in the Northern Hemisphere.

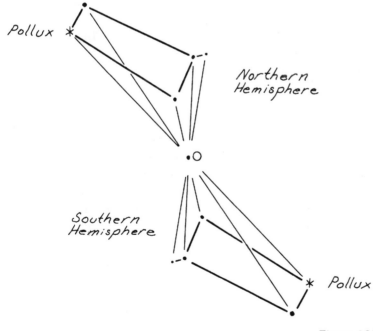

Figure 183

Choosing a point (O), the stars are projected to equal distances on the other side of this point to show how they will appear in the Southern Hemisphere. The oblong shape of the asterism has undergone both a left-right and an up-down inversion.

2.

Similarly, the waxing crescent Moon can be shown for the two hemispheres, as in Figure 184. Notice that the upper cusp of the Moon (A) in the Northern Hemisphere becomes the lower one in the Southern.

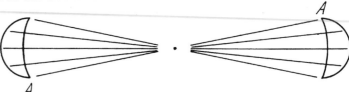

Figure 184

3.

The two hemispheres are inextricably linked yet opposite in their phenomena. One final observation is that the constellation of the Great Bear reaches culmination (i.e., crosses the meridian, a line vertical to the horizon, passing through the poles) at the same local time of day and at the same time of year, as does Crux, the Southern Cross. For example, if the Great Bear reaches upper culmination (passes above the pole) at northern midnight at the end of March, then at southern midnight at the end of March the Southern Cross will also be at upper culmination (discounting seasonal clock changes).

Also, Crux and the Great Bear are virtually the same distance from their poles. The star Acrux is only 1 degree nearer its pole than Dubhe, the leading of the two pointer stars of the Plough. And because the two constellations circle round their poles in opposite ways, they mirror each other in a left-right direction when viewed at the same time of year and local time in their respective hemispheres (Figures 185 and 186). To imagine this, one has to place oneself mentally on each hemisphere alternately, then put the two sky pictures together—readily achieved by consulting planispheres for north and south latitudes.

By this, perhaps, dwellers in both hemispheres can keep aware of each other's starry environment as they separately watch the turning sky.

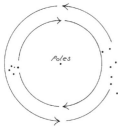

Figure 185

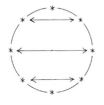

Figure 186

Chapter Ten

The Stars in Poetry

To conclude, I have gathered a number of verses with astronomical content which I have come across over the years, and which may be of use to the teacher or of interest to the general reader. I have also added a few quotations in prose which, in terms of idea, are no less poetic.

The sequence is broadly chronological and may offer some glimpses into the evolution of consciousness and the relationship of the creative mind to science. I have included some comments on the second item, the Egyptian hymn, because I have heard it recited in schools and often wondered what its exact origin was in the hieroglyphic texts. I offer these comments as a preliminary inquiry at least, which may help the teacher to put the verse in context, since I understand it to be an imaginative adaption from the Book of the Dead and not a translation.

COSMIC MAN

A thousand-headed is the Man
with a thousand eyes, a thousand feet;
encompassing the Earth all sides,
he exceeded it by ten fingers' breadth.

The Man, indeed, is this All,
what has been and what is to be,
the Lord of the immortal spheres
which he surpasses by consuming food.

Such is the measure of his might,
and greater still than this is Man.
All beings are a fourth of him,
three fourths are the immortal in heaven.

Three fourths of Man ascended high,
one fourth took birth again down here.
From this he spread in all directions
into animate and inanimate things.

From him the Shining one was born;
from this Shining one Man again took birth.
As soon as born, he extended himself
all over the Earth both behind and before.

. . . . .

When they divided up the Man,
into how many parts did they divide him?
What did his mouth become: What his arms?
What are his legs called? What his feet?

His mouth became the brahmin; his arms
became the warrior-prince, his legs
the common man who plies his trade.
The lowly serf was born from his feet.

The Moon was born from his mind; the Sun
came into being from his eye;
from his mouth came Indra and Agni,
while from his breath the Wind was born.

From his navel issued the Air;
from his head unfurled the Sky,
the Earth from his feet, from his ear the four directions.
Thus have the worlds been organized.

From the hymn *Purusa* (Primordial or Cosmic Man) in the Rig Veda of
ancient India. The Shining one is Viraj, sometimes rendered as "the
cosmic waters," "the cosmic egg," or "the Mother principle." Indra is the
divine warrior whose weapon is the thunderbolt. Agni is the god of the
fire of sacrifice and the divine Fire, and a mediator between Men and
Gods.

* * * * *

THE DEAD MAN ARISETH AND SINGETH
A HYMN TO THE SUN

Homage to thee, O Ra, at thy tremendous rising!
Thou risest! Thou shinest! the heavens are rolled aside!
Thou art the King of Gods, thou art the All-comprising,
From thee we come, in thee are deified.

Thy priests go forth at dawn; they wash their hearts
  with laughter;
Divine winds move in music across thy golden strings.
At sunset they embrace thee, as every cloudy rafter
Flames with reflected color from thy wings.

Thou sailest over the zenith, and thy heart rejoices;
Thy Morning Boat and Evening Boat with fair winds
  meet together;
Before thy face the goddess Maat exalts her fateful
  Feather,
And at thy name the halls of Anu ring with voices.

O Thou Perfect! Thou Eternal! Thou Only One!
Great Hawk that fliest with the flying Sun!
Between the Turquoise Sycamores that risest, young
  for ever,
Thine image flashing on the bright celestial river.

Thy rays are on all faces; Thou art inscrutable.
Age after age thy life renews its eager prime.
Time whirls its dust beneath thee; thou art immutable,
Maker of Time, thyself beyond all Time.

Thou passest through the portals that close behind the
  night,
Gladdening the souls of them that lay in sorrow.
The True of Word, the Quiet Heart, arise to drink thy
  light;
Thou art To-day and Yesterday; Thou art To-morrow!

Homage to thee, O Ra, who wakest life from slumber!
Thou risest! Thou shinest! Thy radiant face appears!
Millions of years have passed,—we can not count their
        number,—
Millions of years shall come. Thou art above the years!

This is a poetic rendering of material from the Egyptian Book of the
Dead. The author is Robert Hillyer (1895–1961), an American poet. In
the 2nd millennium B.C., the Book of the Dead took the form of hiero-
glyphics and pictures on papyri which were laid in the tombs and
which described the "Coming Forth [or Ascension] by Day" of the
deceased in the spirit. The texts seem as much a guide and support for
the departed as a description of their spiritual progress. They were
often written as if they had been spoken by the individual after death,
and some were accompanied by instructions for their recital, etc., by
those surviving the deceased.

Robert Hillyer's verse may well derive its images from Hymns to Ra
found in various tombs, though it has certain similarities with such
Hymns (three of them) in the papyrus for the royal scribe Ani of Thebes
(c. 1420 B.C.). In the verse, Ra (or Re) is the Sun god. Anu is the abode
of the blessed. Maat is the goddess of truth, order, and justice, and the
daughter of Ra. She it was who ordered the daily course of the Sun and
sat in the Judgement Hall of Osiris where the hearts of the dead were
weighed against, and had to balance, the feather of Maat, which she
often wore in her hair. After a night of traveling, during which the heart
was weighed, an individual could not achieve the "Ascension by Day"
itself unless the heart had balanced with the feather.

The picture above the verse I have added from the papyrus of Ani
after he sings a "Hymn of Praise to Ra when he Riseth in the Eastern
Part of Heaven" (Chapter XV) and on having achieved his "Ascension by
Day". It shows Ani on the left praising Ra, who has the head of a hawk
with the Sun disc above him and displays the ankh (ansate cross), the
so-called "symbol of life." Ra is seated on the emblem of maat (qualities
associated with the goddess Maat) and the boat is resting on the sky.

* * * * *

INVOCATION

They are lying down, the great ones.
The bolts are fallen; the fastenings are placed.
The crowds and people are quiet.
The open gates are (now) closed.
The gods of the land and the goddesses of the land,
Shamash, Sin, Adad, and Ishtar,
Have betaken themselves to sleep in heaven.
They are not pronouncing judgement;
They are not deciding things.
Veiled is the night;

The temple and the most holy places are quiet and dark.
The traveller calls on (his) god;
And the litigant is tarrying in sleep.
The judge of the truth, the father of the fatherless,
Shamash, has betaken himself to his chamber.
O great ones, gods of the night,
O bright one, Gibil, O warrior Irra,
O bow (star) and yoke (star),
O pleiades, Orion, and the dragon,
O Ursa major, goat (star), and the bison,
Stand by, and then,
In the divination which I am making,
In the lamb which I am offering,
Put truth for me.

Prayer before a divination ceremony. Babylonian, second millennium
B.C. Shamash is the god of the Sun, Sin is the Moon, Adad is a
weather god, Ishtar is the goddess of the planet Venus, Gibil is the
god of fire, and Irra is a storm god.

* * * * *

PSALM OF DAVID

The heavens declare the glory of God; and the firmament
sheweth his handywork.

Day unto day uttereth speech, and night unto night
sheweth knowledge.

There is no speech nor language, where their voice is not
heard.

Their line is gone out through all the earth, and their
words to the end of the world. In them hath he set a taberna-
cle for the sun,

Which is as a bridegroom coming out of his chamber, and
rejoiceth as a strong man to run a race.

His going forth is from the end of the heaven, and his circuit unto the ends of it: and there is nothing hid from the
heat thereof.

From the Old Testament, Psalm 19;
a Psalm of David, to the chief Musician.

* * * * *

When the Pleiads, Atlas' daughters, start to rise
Begin your harvest; plough when they go down.
For forty days and nights they hide themselves,
And as the year rolls round, appear again
When you begin to sharpen sickle-blades;
This law holds on the plains and by the sea,
And in the mountain valleys, fertile lands
Far from the swelling sea.

From *Works and Days*
by Hesiod (c. 8th century B.C.)

* * * * *

To one who asked why he was alive, Empedocles
replied, "That I may behold the stars; take away the
firmament, I will be nothing."

From *Cosmographia*
by Bernardus Silvestris (12th century A.D.)

(Empedocles lived c. 450 B.C.)

* * * * *

And when he [the author of the universe] had compounded the
whole, he divided it up into as many souls as there are stars,
and allotted each soul to a star. And mounting them on their
stars, as if on chariots, he showed them the nature of the universe and told them the laws of their destiny.

From *Timaeus* by Plato (c. 427–347 B.C.)

* * * * *

....the cause and purpose of god's invention and gift to us
of sight was that we should see the revolutions of intelligence
in the heavens and use their untroubled course to guide the
troubled revolutions in our own understanding, which are

akin to them, and so, by learning what they are and how to calculate them accurately according to their nature, correct the disorder of our own revolutions by the standard of the invariability of those of god.

From *Timaeus* by Plato

* * * * *

TO STELLA

Thou wert the morning star among the living,
    Ere thy fair light had fled;
Now, having died, thou art as Hesperus, giving
    New splendour to the dead.

An epigram by Percy Bysshe Shelley,
taken from the Greek of Plato.

Venus was called Hesperus by the Greeks when it was an evening star.

* * * * *

Now near the Twins behold Orion rise;
His arms extended measure half the skies:
His stride no less. Onward with steady pace
He treads the boundless realms of starry space,
On each broad shoulder a bright star display'd,
And three obliquely grace his hanging blade.
In his vast head, immers'd in boundless spheres,
Three stars less bright, but yet as great, he bears;
But farther off removed, their splendour's lost;
Thus grac'd and arm'd, he leads the starry host.

From *Astronomica*
by Manilius (1st century A.D.)

* * * * *

I know I am mortal, a creature of the day;
Yet in spirit I accompany the wandering stars as they
    circle round the Pole,
Though my foot no longer touches the earth. By the
    side of Zeus himself
I share the meal which preserves the Gods themselves in
    immortality.

> Epitaph, by himself,
> of Ptolemy (2nd century A.D.)

* * * * *

Wake! for the Sun, who scatter'd into flight
The stars before him from the Field of Night,
  Drives night along with them from Heav'n and strikes
The Sultan's Turret with a Shaft of Light.

> From the *Rubaiyat* of Omar Khayyam (c. 1050–1123)

* * * * *

As the geometer his mind applies
    To square the circle, nor for all his wit
    Finds the right formula, howe'er he tries,

So strove I with that wonder—how to fit
    The image to the sphere; so sought to see
    How it maintained the point of rest in it.

Thither my own wings could not carry me,
    But that a flash my understanding clove,
    Whence its desire came to it suddenly.

High phantasy lost power and here broke off;
    Yet, as a wheel moves smoothly, free from jars,
    My will and my desire were turned by love,

The love that moves the sun and the other stars.

> The last stanza of *Paradiso*
> by Dante Alighieri (1265–1321)

* * * * *

Our Hoste saw that in heven the brighte sonne
Of his artificial day the arke had ronne
The fourthe part, of half an hour and more;
And though he were not deep expert in lore,
He wist it was the eightetenthe day
Of April, that is messanger to May;
And saw wel that the shade of every tree
Was in the lengthe the same quantitee
That was the body erecte, that causèd it;
And therefore by the shadwe he took wit,
That Phebus, which that shoon so fair and brighte,
Degrees was five and fourty clombe on highte;
And for that day, as in that latitude,
It was ten of the clok, he gan conclude; . . .

From *Canterbury Tales* ("The Man of Lawes Tale") by Geoffrey Chaucer (c. 1345–1400). Our Hoste's reasoning is along the lines of calculation with an astrolabe, a medieval astronomical instrument upon which Chaucer wrote a treatise.

* * * * *

I wol yow telle, as was me taught also,
The foure spirites and the bodies sevene,
By ordre, as ofte I herde my lord hem nevene,
The firste spirit quik-silver called is,
The second orpiment, the thridde, y-wis,
Sal armoniak, and the ferthe brimstoon.
The bodies sevene eek, lo! hem heer anoon:
Sol gold is, and Luna silver we threpe,
Mars yren, Mercurie quik-silver we clepe,
Saturnus leed, and Jupiter is tin,
And Venus coper, by my fader kin!

From *Canterbury Tales* ("The Canon's Yeoman's Tale")
by Geoffrey Chaucer

* * * * *

With us ther was a Doctour of Phisyk,
In al this world ne was ther noon him lyk
To speke of phisik and of surgerye;
For he was grounded in astronomye.

From the "Prologue" to *Canterbury Tales*
by Geoffrey Chaucer

* * * * *

FAUSTUS: Come, Mephistophilis, let us dispute again,
And argue of divine astrology.
Tell me, are there many heavens above the
Moon?
Are all celestial bodies but one globe,
As is the substance of this centric earth?

MEPHISTO: As are the elements, such are the spheres,
Mutually folded in each other's orb,
And Faustus,
All jointly move upon one axletree,
Whose terminine is termed the world's
wide pole,
Nor are the names of Saturn, Mars or Jupiter
Feigned, but are erring stars.

FAUSTUS: But tell me, have they all one motion?
Both *situ* and *tempore*?

MEPHISTO: All jointly move from East to West in four
and twenty hours upon the poles of the
world, but differ in their motion upon the
poles of the zodiac.

FAUSTUS: Tush, these slender trifles Wagner can
decide,
Hath Mephistophilis no greater skill?
Who knows not the double motion of the
planets?
The first is finished in a natural day,
The second thus, as Saturn in thirty years,
Jupiter in twelve, Mars in four, the Sun,
Venus, and Mercury in a year: the Moon

in twenty-eight days. Tush, these are fresh-
men's suppositions; but tell me, hath every
sphere a Dominion or *Intelligentia*?

MEPHISTO: Aye.

FAUSTUS: How many heavens or spheres are there?

MEPHISTO: Nine, the seven planets, the Firmament,
and the Empyrean Heaven.

FAUSTUS: But is there not *Coelum Igneum and Christa-
linum*?

MEPHISTO: No, Faustus, they be but fables.

FAUSTUS: Well, resolve me in this question, why have
we not conjunctions, oppositions, aspects,
eclipses, all at one time, but in some years
we have more, in some less?

MEPHISTO: *Per inaequalem motum respectu totius.**

FAUSTUS: Well, I am answered; tell me, who made
the world?

MEPHISTO: I will not.

FAUSTUS: Sweet Mephistophilis, tell me.

MEPHISTO: Move me not, for I will not tell thee.

FAUSTUS: Villain, have I not bound thee to tell me
anything?

MEPHISTO: Aye, that is not against our kingdom, but
this is.
Think thou on hell, Faustus, for thou art
damned.

From *Doctor Faustus*
by Christopher Marlowe (1564–1593)

* By the inequality of their movement in reference to the whole.

* * * * *

The heavens themselves, the planets, and
    this centre,
Observe degree, priority, and place,
Insisture, course, proportion, season, form,
Office, and custom, in all line of order;
And therefore is the glorious planet Sol
In noble eminence enthron'd and spher'd
Amidst the other, whose med'cinable eye
Corrects the ill aspects of planets evil,
And posts, like the commandment of a
    king,
Sans check, to good and bad. But when the
    planets
In evil mixture to disorder wander,
What plagues and what portents, what
    mutiny,
What raging of the sea, shaking of earth,
Commotion in the winds! Frights, changes,
    horrors,
Divert and crack, rend and deracinate,
The unity and married calm of states
Quite from their fixture!

From *Troilus and Cressida*
by William Shakespeare (1564–1616)

* * * * *

But I am constant as the northern star,
Of whose true-fix'd and resting quality
There is no fellow in the firmament.
The skies are painted with unnumb'red
    sparks,
They are all fire, and every one doth shine;
But there's but one in all doth hold his
    place.

From *Julius Caesar*
by William Shakespeare

* * * * *

Men at some time are masters of their fates:
The fault, dear Brutus, is not in our stars,
But in ourselves, that we are underlings.

From *Julius Caesar*
by William Shakespeare

* * * * *

When beggars die there are no
    comets seen:
The heavens themselves blaze forth the
    death of princes.

From *Julius Caesar*
by William Shakespeare

* * * * *

JULIET: O, swear not by the moon, th' inconstant moon,
That monthly changes in her circled orb,
Lest that thy love prove likewise variable.

From *Romeo and Juliet*
by William Shakespeare

* * * * *

Love is not love
Which alters when it alteration finds,
Or bends with the remover to remove.
O, no! it is an ever-fixed mark,
That looks on tempests and is never shaken;
It is the star to every wand'ring bark,
Whose worth's unknown, although his
    height be taken.

From *Sonnet No. 116*
by William Shakespeare

* * * * *

And new Philosophy calls all in doubt,
The Element of fire is quite put out;
The Sun is lost, and th'earth, and no man's wit
Can well direct him where to looke for it.
And freely men confesse that this world's spent,
When in the Planets, and the Firmament
They seeke so many new; then see that this
Is crumbled out againe to his Atomies.
'Tis all in peeces, all cohaerence gone;
All just supply, and all Relation:
Prince, Subject, Father, Sonne, are things forgot,
For every man alone thinkes he hath got
To be a Phoenix, and that then can bee
None of that kinde, of which he is, but hee.

· · · · ·

We thinke the heavens enjoy their Sphericall,
Their round proportion embracing all.
But yet their various and perplexed course,
Observ'd in divers ages, doth enforce
Men to finde out so many Eccentrique parts,
Such divers downe-right lines, such overthwarts,
As disproportion that pure forme: It teares
The Firmament in eight and forty sheires,
And in these Constellations then arise
New starres, and old doe vanish from our eyes:
As though heav'n suffered earthquakes, peace or
         war,
When new Towers rise, and old demolish't are.
They have impal'd within a Zodiake
The free-borne Sun, and keepe twelve Signes awake
To watch his steps; the Goat and Crab controule,
And fright him backe, who else to either Pole
(Did not these Tropiques fetter him) might runne:
For his course is not round; nor can the Sunne
Perfit a Circle, or maintaine his way
One inch direct; but where he rose to-day
He comes no more, but with a couzening line,
Steales by that point, and so is Serpentine:
And seeming weary with his reeling thus,
He meanes to sleepe, being now falne nearer us.
So, of the Starres which boast that they doe runne
In Circle still, none ends where he begun.

All their proportion's lame, it sinkes, it swels.
For of Meridians, and Parallels,
Man hath weav'd out a net, and this net throwne
Upon the Heavens, and now they are his owne.
Loth to goe up the hill, or labour thus
To goe to heaven, we make heaven come to us.
We spur, we reine the starres, and in their race
They're diversly content t'obey our pace.

From <i>An Anatomie of the World: The First Anniversary</i>
by John Donne (1571–1631)

* * * * *

We do not ask for what useful purpose the birds do sing, for song is their pleasure since they were created for singing. Similarly, we ought not to ask why the human mind troubles to fathom the secrets of the heavens.... The diversity of the phenomena of Nature is so great, and the treasures hidden in the heavens so rich, precisely in order that the human mind shall never be lacking in fresh nourishment.

From his dedication to his book <i>Mysterium Cosmographicum</i> by
Johannes Kepler (1571–1630)

* * * * *

...if there is anything that can bind the heavenly mind of man to this dusty exile of our earthly home and can reconcile us with our fate so that one can enjoy living—then it is verily the enjoyment of...the mathematical sciences and astronomy.

From a letter to his son-in-law Jacob Bartsch,
by Johannes Kepler

* * * * *

Mensus Eram Coelos Nunc
Terrae Metior Umbras
Mens Coelestis Erat
Corporis Umbra Iacet

[Once I measured the skies,
 Now I measure the earth's shadow.
 Of heavenly birth was the measuring mind,
 In the shadow remains only the body.]

Johannes Kepler's self–written epitaph
on his original tombstone at Regensburg

* * * * *

Although there were some fourtie
            heav'ns, or more,
    Sometimes I peere above them all;
    Sometimes I hardly reach a score,
        Sometimes to hell I fall.

O rack me not to such a vast extent;
    Those distances belong to thee:
    The world's too little for thy tent,
        A grave too big for me.

From *The Temper*
by George Herbert (1593–1633)

* * * * *

The fleet Astronomer can bore,
And thred the spheres with his
            quick-piercing minde:
He views their stations, walks from
            doore to doore,
    Surveys, as if he had design'd
To make a purchase there: he sees their dances,
    And knoweth long before
Both their full-ey'd aspects, and secret glances.

From *Man* by George Herbert

* * * * *

When I survay the bright
    Coelestiall spheare:
So rich with jewels hung, that night
Doth like an Aethiop bride appeare,

    My soule her wings doth spread
      And heaven-ward flies,
Th'Almighty's Mysteries to read
In the large volumes of the skies.

    For the bright firmament
      Shootes forth no flame
So silent, but is eloquent
In speaking the Creators name.

From *Nox nocti indicat Scientiam. DAVID*
by William Habington (1605–1654)

* * * * *

One after one the stars have risen and set,
Sparkling upon the hoar-frost of my chain;
The Bear that prowled all night about the fold
Of the North-star hath shrunk into his den,
Scared by the blithesome footsteps of the Dawn.

By William Habington

* * * * *

The Stars with deep amaze
Stand fixt in stedfast gaze,
  Bending one way their pretious influence,
And will not take their flight,
For all the morning light,
  Or Lucifer that often warn'd them thence;
But in their glimmering Orbs did glow,
Untill their Lord himself bespake, and bid them go.

. . . . .

Ring out ye Crystall sphears,
Once bless our human ears,
  (If ye have power to touch our senses so)
And let your silver chime
Move in melodious time;
  And let the Base of Heav'ns deep Organ blow
And with your ninefold harmony
Make up full consort to th'Angelike symphony.

    . . . . .

So when the Sun in bed,
Curtain'd with cloudy red,
  Pillows his chin upon an Orient wave,
The flocking shadows pale,
Troop to th'infernall jail,
  Each fetter'd Ghost slips to his severall grave,
And the yellow-skirted Fayes,
Fly after the Night-steeds, leaving their Moon-lov'd maze.

From *Hymn on the Morning of Christ's Nativity*
by John Milton. (1608–1674)

* * * * *

Now glowed the firmament
With living sapphires; Hesperus that led
The starry host, rode brightest, till the Moon,
Rising in clouded majesty, at length
Apparent Queen, unveiled her peerless light
And o'er the dark her silver mantle threw.

From *Paradise Lost* by John Milton

* * * *

       ...the grey
Dawn and the *Pleiades* before him danc'd
Shedding sweet influence....

From *Paradise Lost* by John Milton

* * * * *

The Centre of our world's the lively light
Of the warm sunne, the visible Deity
Of this externall Temple. *Mercurie*
Next plac'd and warm'd more thoroughly
     by his rayes,
Right nimbly 'bout his golden head
     doth fly:
Then *Venus* nothing slow about him
     strayes
And next our *Earth* though seeming sad
     full sprightly playes.

From *Democritus Platonissans*
by Henry More (1614–1687)

* * * * *

From harmony, from heavenly harmony,
    This universal frame began:
When nature underneath a heap
    Of jarring atoms lay,
    And could not heave her head,
The tuneful voice was heard from high,
    'Arise, ye more than dead!'
Then cold, and hot, and moist, and dry,
  In order to their stations leap,
    And Music's power obey.
From harmony, from heavenly harmony,
    This universal frame began:
    From harmony to harmony
Through all the compass of the notes it ran,
The diapason closing full in Man.

What passion cannot Music raise and quell?
    When Jubal struck the chorded shell,
  His listening brethren stood around,
    And, wondering, on their faces fell
  To worship that celestial sound:
Less than a God they thought there could not dwell
    Within the hollow of that shell,
    That spoke so sweetly, and so well.
What passion cannot Music raise and quell?

. . . . .

Grand Chorus

As from the power of sacred lays
    The spheres began to move,
And sung the great Creator's praise
    To all the Blest above;
So when the last and dreadful hour
This crumbling pageant shall devour,
The trumpet shall be heard on high,
The dead shall live, the living die,
And Music shall untune the sky!

From *A Song for St. Cecilia's Day, 1687*
by John Dryden (1631–1700)

* * * * *

The Thoughts of Men appear
Freely to mov within a Sphere
    Of endless Reach; and run,
Tho in the Soul, beyond the Sun.
The Ground on which they acted be
Is unobserv'd Infinity.

From *Consummation*
by Thomas Traherne (c. 1636–1674)

* * * * *

The spacious firmament on high,
With all the blue ethereal sky,
And spangled heavens, a shining frame,
Their great Original proclaim.
Th' unwearied Sun from day to day
Does his Creator's power display;
And publishes to every land
The work of an Almighty hand.

Soon as the evening shades prevail,
The Moon takes up the wondrous tale;
And nightly to the listening Earth

Repeats the story of her birth:
Whilst all the stars that round her burn,
And all the planets in their turn,
Confirm the tidings as they roll,
And spread the truth from pole to pole.

From *Hymn* by Joseph Addison (1672–1719)

* * * * *

The Ram, the Bull, the Heavenly Twins
And next the Crab, the Lion shines,
    The Virgin and the Scales,
The Scorpion, Archer and Sea Goat,
The Man who held the Watering Pot
    And Fishes with glittering tails.

By Isaac Watts (1674–1748).

* * * * *

Devotion! Daughter of Astronomy,
An undevout Astronomer is mad.

From *Night Thoughts*
by Edward Young (1685–1765)

* * * * *

But never yet did philosophic tube,
That brings the planets home into the eye
Of Observation, and discovers, else
Not visible, his family of worlds,
Discover him, that rules them; such a veil
Hangs over mortal eyes, blind from the birth,
And dark in things divine. Full often too
Our wayward intellect, the more we learn
Of nature, overlooks her Author more; . . .

From *The Task*, Book 3,
by William Cowper (1731–1800)

* * * * *

RAPHAEL: The chanting sun, as ever, rivals
　　　　　　The chanting of his brother spheres
　　　　　　And marches round his destined circuit—
　　　　　　A march that thunders in our ears.
　　　　　　His aspect cheers the Hosts of Heaven
　　　　　　Though what his essence none can say;
　　　　　　These inconceivable creations
　　　　　　Keep the high state of their first day.

From *Faust*, Part 1 ("Prologue in Heaven")
by Johann Wolfgang von Goethe (1749–1832)

* * * * *

TO THE EVENING STAR

Thou fair-haired Angel of the Evening,
Now, whilst the sun rests on the mountains,
　　　light
Thy bright torch of love—thy radiant crown
Put on, and smile upon our evening bed!
Smile on our loves; and, while thou drawest the
Blue curtains of the sky, scatter thy silver dew
On every flower that shuts its sweet eyes
In timely sleep. Let thy west wind sleep on
The lake; speak silence with thy glimmering eyes,
And wash the dusk with silver. Soon, full soon,
Dost thou withdraw; then the wolf rages wide,
And the lion glares through the dun forest.
The fleeces of our flocks are covered with
Thy sacred dew: protect them with thine influence!

By William Blake (1757–1827).

* * * * *

The sun descending in the west,
　　The evening star does shine;
The birds are silent in their nest,
　　And I must seek for mine.
　　　　The moon, like a flower
　　　　In heaven's high bower,
　　　　With silent delight
　　　　Sits and smiles on the night.

From *Night* by William Blake.

* * * * *

TO MORNING

O Holy virgin, clad in purest white,
Unlock heaven's golden gates, and issue forth;
Awake the dawn that sleeps in heaven; let light
Rise from the chambers of the east, and bring
The honeyed dew that cometh on waking day.
O radiant Morning, salute the Sun,
Roused like a huntsman to the chase, and with
Thy buskined feet appear upon our hills.

By William Blake.

* * * * *

The Sun's rim dips; the stars rush out:
At one stride comes the dark;

. . . . .

The moving Moon went up the sky,
And nowhere did abide;
Softly she was going up,
And a star or two beside—

From *The Rime of the Ancient Mariner*
by Samuel Taylor Coleridge (1772–1834).

* * * * *

It is no Spirit who from heaven hath flown,
And is decending on his embassy;
Nor Traveller gone from earth the heavens to espy!
'Tis Hesperus—there he stands with glittering
      crown,
First admonition that the sun is down!
For yet it is broad day-light: clouds pass by;
A few are near him still— and now the sky,
He hath it to himself—'t is all his own.
O most ambitious Star! an inquest wrought
Within me when I recognised thy light;
A moment I was startled at the sight:
And, while I gazed, there came to me a thought
That I might step beyond my natural race
As thou seem'st now to do; might one day trace
Some ground not mine; and, strong her
      strength above,
My Soul, an Apparition in the place,
Tread there with steps that no one shall reprove!

By William Wordsworth (1770–1850). Hesperus was a name given to
the planet Venus as evening star. Wordsworth wrote of this poem:
"Written at Town-end, Grasmere. I remember the instant my sister,
S.H., called me to the window of our Cottage, saying, 'Look how
beautiful is yon star! It has the sky all to itself.' I composed the
verses immediately."

* * * * *

Ye stars! which are the poetry of heaven!
If in your bright leaves we would read the fate
Of men and empires—'tis to be forgiven
That in our aspirations to be great,
Our destinies o'erleap their mortal state
And claim a kindred with you; for ye are
A beauty and a mystery, and create
In us such love and reverence from afar,
That fortune, fame, power, life, have named themselves
     a star.

From *Childe Harold's Pilgrimage*
by Byron (1788–1824)

* * * * *

TO THE MOON

Art thou pale for weariness
Of climbing heaven and gazing on the earth,
　　Wandering companionless
Among the stars that have a different birth,
And ever changing, like a joyless eye
That finds no object worth its constancy?

By Percy Bysshe Shelley (1792–1822)

* * * * *

Palace-Roof of cloudless nights!
Paradise of golden lights!
　　Deep, immeasurable, vast,
Which art now, and which wert
　　　　then
　　Of the Present and the Past,
Of the eternal Where and When,
　　Presence-chamber, temple, home,
　　Ever-canopying dome,
　　Of acts and ages yet to come!

· · · · ·

What is Heaven? a globe of dew,
Filling in the morning new
　　Some eyed flower whose young
　　　　leaves waken
On an unimagined world:
　　Constellated suns unshaken,
Orbits measureless, are furled
　　In that frail and fading sphere,
　　With ten millions gathered
　　　　there,
　　To tremble, gleam, and disappear.

From *Ode to Heaven* by Percy Bysshe Shelley

* * * * *

Swiftly walk over the western wave,
Spirit of Night!
Out of the misty eastern cave,
Where, all the long and lone daylight,
Thou wovest dreams of joy and fear,
Which make thee terrible and dear,—
Swift be thy flight!

From *To Night*
by Percy Bysshe Shelley

* * * * *

Constellations come, and climb the heavens, and go,
And thou dost see them rise,
Star of the Pole! and thou dost see them set.
Alone, in thy cold skies,
Thou keep'st thy old unmoving station yet.

From *Hymn to the North Star*
by William Cullen Bryant (1794–1878)

* * * * *

When, as the garish day is done,
Heaven burns with the descended sun,
'Tis passing sweet to mark,
Amid that flush of crimson light,
The new moon's modest bow grow bright,
As earth and sky grow dark.

From *The New Moon*
by William Cullen Bryant

* * * * *

See where upon the horizon's brim,
    Lies the still cloud in gloomy bars;
The waning moon, all pale and dim,
    Goes up amid the eternal stars.

From *The Waning Moon* by William Cullen Bryant

* * * * *

If the stars should appear one night in a thousand years, how would men believe and adore and preserve for many generations the remembrance of the city of God which had been shown?

By Ralph Waldo Emerson (1803–1882)

* * * * *

Can it be the sun descending
O'er the level plain of water?
Or the Red Swan floating, flying,
Wounded by the magic arrow,
Staining all the waves with crimson,
With the crimson of its life-blood,
Filling all the air with splendour,
With the splendour of its plumage?
    Yes; it is the sun descending,
Sinking down into the water;
All the sky is stained with purple,
All the water flushed with crimson!
No; it is the Red Swan floating,
Diving down beneath the water;
To the sky its wings are lifted,
With its blood the waves are reddened!
    Over it the Star of Evening
Melts and trembles through the purple,
Hangs suspended in the twilight.
No; it is a bead of wampum
On the robes of the Great Spirit,
As he passes through the twilight,
Walks in silence through the heavens!

From *The Song of Hiawatha* by Henry Longfellow (1807–1882).

* * * * *

Many a night from yonder ivied casement, ere I went to rest,
Did I look on great Orion sloping slowly to the West.

Many a night I saw the Pleiads, rising thro' the mellow shade,
Glitter like a swarm of fire-flies tangled in a silver braid.

From *Locksley Hall*
by Alfred Tennyson (1809–1892)

* * * * *

THE ASTRONOMER

1

Upon thy lofty tower,
  O lonely Sage,
Reading at midnight hour
  Heaven's awful page!
Thine art can poise the sun
  In balance true,
And countless worlds that run
  Beyond our view.
Thou scannest with clear eyes
  The azure cope;
To thee the galaxies
  Their secrets ope;
Thou know'st the track sublime
  Of every star;
Space infinite, and Time,
  Thy problems are.
O Sage! whose mental span
  Thus grasps the sky,
How great the soul of man
  That soars so high!

2

But yet thou canst not guess,
  With all thy skill,
What seas of happiness
  My bosom fill.

Thou canst not track the woe,
   The hope, the faith,
That prompt the ebb and flow
   Of my poor breath.
Outspeeding with thy thought
   The solar ray,
Thou canst not, knowledge-fraught,
   Discern my way.
My love—its depth and height,—
   Thou canst not sound;
Nor of my guilt's dark night
   Pierce the profound.
O student of the sky
   My pride departs;
Worlds undiscover'd lie
   In both our hearts!

From *Songs for Music*
by Charles Mackay (1814–1889)

* * * * *

WHEN I HEARD THE LEARN'D ASTRONOMER

When I heard the learn'd astronomer,
When the proofs, the figures, were ranged in columns
    before me,
When I was shown the charts and diagrams, to add,
    divide, and measure them,
When I sitting heard the astronomer where he lectured
    with much applause in the lecture-room,
How soon unaccountable I became tired and sick,
Till rising and gliding out I wander'd off by myself,
In the mystical moist night-air, and from time to time,
Look'd up in perfect silence at the stars.

By Walt Whitman (1819–1891)

* * * * *

MEDITATION UNDER STARS

What links are ours with orbs that are
　　So resolutely far:
The solitary asks, and they
Give radiance as from a shield:
　　　Still at the death of day,
　　　The seen, the unrevealed.
　　　Implacable they shine
To us who would of Life obtain
An answer for the life we strain
　　To nourish with one sign.
Nor can imagination throw
The penetrative shaft: we pass
The breath of thought, who would divine
　　If haply they may grow
As Earth; have our desire to know;
If life comes there to grain from grass,
And flowers like ours of toil and pain;
　　　Has passion to beat bar,
　　　Win space from cleaving brain;
　　　The mystic link attain,
　　　Whereby star holds on star.

. . . . .

So may we read, and little find them cold:
Not frosty lamps illumining dead space,
Not distant aliens, not senseless Powers.
The fire is in them whereof we are born;
The music of their motion may be ours.
Spirit shall deem them beckoning Earth and voiced
Sisterly to her, in her beams rejoiced.
Of love, the grand impulsion, we behold
　　The love that lends her grace
　　Among the starry fold.
Then at new flood of customary morn,
　　Look at her through her showers,
　　Her mists, her streaming gold,
A wonder edges the familiar face:
She wears no more that robe of printed hours;
Half strange seems Earth, and sweeter than her flowers.

From *A Reading of Earth* by George Meredith (1828–1909)

* * * * *

WINTER HEAVENS

Sharp is the night, but stars with frost alive
Leap off the rim of earth across the dome.
It is a night to make the heavens our home
More than the nest whereto apace we strive.
Lengths down our road each fir-tree seems a hive,
Its swarms outrushing from the golden comb.
They waken waves of thoughts that burst to foam:
The living throb in me, the dead revive.
Yon mantle clothes us: there, past mortal breath,
Life glistens on the river of the death.
It folds us, flesh and dust; and have we knelt,
Or never knelt, or eyed as kine the springs
Of radiance, the radiance enrings:
And this is the soul's haven to have felt.

By George Meredith

* * * * *

Is the moon tired? she looks so pale
Within her misty veil:
She scales the sky from east to west,
And takes no rest.

Before the coming of the night
The moon shows papery white;
Before the dawning of the day
She fades away.

From *Sing-Song* by Christina Rossetti (1830–1894)

* * * * *

O Lady Moon, your horns point toward the east;
Shine, be increased:
O Lady Moon, your horns point toward the west;
Wane, be at rest.

From *Sing-Song* by Christina Rossetti

* * * * *

THE HALF MOON SHOWS
A FACE OF PLAINTIVE SWEETNESS

The half moon shows a face of plaintive sweetness
    Ready and poised to wax or wane;
A fire of pale desire in incompleteness,
    Tending to pleasure or to pain:—
Lo, while we gaze she rolleth on in fleetness
    To perfect loss or perfect gain.
Half bitterness we know, we know half sweetness;
    This world is all on wax, on wane:
When shall completeness round time's incompleteness,
    Fulfilling joy, fulfilling pain?—
Lo, while we ask, life rolleth on in fleetness
    To finished loss or finished gain.

By Christina Rossetti

* * * * *

THE APPOINTMENT

'Tis late; the astronomer in his lonely height,
Exploring all the dark, descries afar
Orbs that like distant isles of splendour are,
And mornings whitening in the infinite.

Like winnowed grain the worlds go by in flight,
Or swarm in glistening spaces nebular;
He summons one dishevelled wandering star,—
Return ten centuries hence on such a night.

The star will come. It dare not by one hour
Cheat Science, or falsify her calculation;
Men will have passed, but watchful in the tower

Man shall remain in sleepless contemplation;
And should all men have perished there in turn,
Truth in their place would watch that star's return.

By Sully Prudhomme (1839–1907)

* * * * *

AT A LUNAR ECLIPSE

Thy shadow, Earth, from Pole to Central Sea,
Now steals along upon the Moon's meek shine
In even monochrome and curving line
Of imperturbable serenity.

How shall I link such sun-cast symmetry
With the torn troubled form I know as thine,
That profile, placid as a brow divine,
With continents of moil and misery?

And can immense Mortality but throw
So small a shade, and Heaven's high human scheme
Be hemmed within the coasts yon arc implies?

Is such the stellar gauge of earthly show,
Nation at war with nation, brains that teem,
Heroes, and women fairer than the skies?

By Thomas Hardy (1840–1928)

* * * * *

THE STARLIGHT NIGHT

Look at the stars! look, look up at the skies!
  O look at all the fire-folk sitting in the air!
  The bright boroughs, the circle-citadels there!
Down in dim woods the diamond delves! the elves'-eyes!

The grey lawns cold where gold, where quickgold lies!
  Wind-beat whitebeam! airy abeles set on a flare!
  Flake-doves sent floating forth at a farmyard scare!—
Ah well! it is all a purchase, all is a prize.

Buy then! bid then!—What?—Prayer, patience, alms, vows.
Look, look: a May-mess, like on orchard boughs!
  Look! March-bloom, like on mealed-with-yellow sallows!
These are indeed the barn; withindoors house
The shocks. This piece-bright paling shuts the spouse
  Christ home, Christ and his mother and all his hallows.

By Gerard Manley Hopkins (1844–1889)

* * * * *

STAR MORALS

Called a star's orbit to pursue,
What is the darkness, star, to you?

Roll on in bliss, traverse this age—
Its misery far from you and strange.

Let farthest world your light secure.
Pity is sin you must abjure.

But one command is yours: be pure!

By Friedrich Nietzsche (1844–1900)

* * * * *

One night I went for a walk by the sea along the empty shore. It was not gay, but neither was it sad—it was—beautiful. The deep blue sky was flecked with clouds of a blue deeper than the fundamental blue of intense cobalt, and others of a clearer blue, like the blue whiteness of the Milky Way. In the blue depth the stars were sparkling, greenish, yellow, white, rose, brighter, flashing more like jewels, than they do at home—even in Paris: opals you might call them, emeralds, lapis, rubies, sapphires.

From a letter by Vincent van Gogh (1853–1890)
written from Saintes-Maries-sur-Mer in June, 1888, to his brother Theo.

* * * * *

.... to look at the stars always makes me dream, *as simply* as I dream over the black dots of a map representing towns and villages. Why, I ask myself, should the shining dots of the sky not be as accessible as the black dots on the map of France? If we take the train to get to Tarascon or Rouen, we take death to reach a star. One thing undoubtedly true in this reasoning is this, that while we are *alive* we *cannot* get to a star, any more than when we are dead we can take the train.

From a letter by Vincent van Gogh
written from Arles in July, 1888, to his brother Theo.

* * * * *

When to the new eyes of thee
All things by immortal power,
Near or far,
Hiddenly
To each other linked are,
That thou canst not stir a flower
Without troubling of a star;
.....seek no more,...

From *The Mistress of Vision*
by Francis Thompson (1859–1907)

* * * * *

The Stars spake once to Man.
It is World-destiny
That they are silent now.
To be aware of the silence
Can become pain for earthly Man.

But in the deepening silence
There grows and ripens
What Man speaks to the Stars.
To be aware of the speaking
Can become strength for Spirit-Man.

By Rudolf Steiner (1861–1925)

* * * * *

If to the heavens you lift your eyes
When Winter reigns o'er our Northern skies,
And snow-cloud none the zenith mars,
At Yule-tide midnight these your stars:
Low in the South see bleak-blazing Sirius;
Above him hang Betelgeuse, Procyon wan;
Wild-eyed to West of him, Rigel and Bellatrix,
And rudd-red Aldebaran journeying on.
High in night's roof-tree beams twinkling Capella;
Vega and Deneb prowl low in the North;
Far to the East roves the Lion-heart, Regulus;
While the twin sons of Zeus to'rd the zenith gleam forth.

But when Midsummer Eve in man's sleep-drowsed hours
Refreshes for daybreak its dew-bright flowers,
Though three of these Night Lights aloft remain,
For nine, if you gaze, you will gaze in vain.
Yet comfort find, for, far-shining there,
See golden Arcturus and cold Altair;
Crystalline Spica, and, strange to scan,
Blood-red Antares, foe to Man.

From *Stars* by Walter de la Mare (1873–1956)

* * * * *

WANDERERS

Wide are the meadows of night,
And daisies are shining there,
Tossing their lovely dews,
Lustrous and fair;
And through these sweet fields go,
Wand'rers 'mid the stars—
Venus, Mercury, Uranus, Neptune,
Saturn, Jupiter, Mars.

'Tired in their silver, they move,
And circling, whisper and say,
Fair are the blossoming meads of delight
Through which we stray.

By Walter de la Mare

* * * * *

FULL MOON

One night as Dick lay fast asleep,
    Into his drowsy eyes
A great still light began to creep
    From out the silent skies.
It was the lovely moon's, for when
    He raised his dreamy head,
Her surge of silver filled the pane
    And streamed across his bed.
So, for a while, each gazed at each—
    Dick and the solemn moon—
Till, climbing slowly on her way,
    She vanished, and was gone.

By Walter de la Mare

* * * * *

Oh, it was wild and weird and wan, and ever in
    camp o' nights
We would watch and watch the silver dance of the
    mystic Northern Lights.
And soft they danced from the Polar sky and
    swept in primrose haze;
And swift they pranced with their silver feet, and
    pierced with a blinding blaze.
They danced a cotillion in the sky; they were
    rose and silver shod;
It was not good for the eyes of man—'twas a sight
    for the eyes of God.
It made us mad and strange and sad, and the
    gold whereof we dreamed
Was all forgot, and our only thought was of the
    lights that gleamed.

From "The Ballad of the Northern Lights"
in *Ballads of a Cheechako* by Robert Service (1874–1958)

* * * * *

CHOOSE SOMETHING LIKE A STAR

O Star (the fairest one in sight),
We grant your loftiness the right
To some obscurity of cloud—
It will not do to say of night,
Since dark is what brings out your light.
Some mystery becomes the proud.
But to be wholly taciturn
In your reserve is not allowed.
Say something to us we can learn
By heart and when alone repeat.
Say something! And it says "I burn."
But say with what degree of heat.
Talk Fahrenheit, talk Centigrade.
Use language we can comprehend.
Tell us what elements you blend.
It gives us strangely little aid,
But does tell something in the end.
And steadfast as Keats' Eremite,
Not even stooping from its sphere,
It asks a little of us here.
It asks of us a certain height,
So when at times the mob is swayed
To carry praise or blame too far,
We may choose something like a star
To stay our minds on and be staid.

By Robert Frost (1874–1963)

* * * * *

"You know Orion always comes up sideways.
Throwing a leg up over our fence of mountains,
And rising on his hands, he looks in on me
Busy outdoors by lantern-light with something
I should have done by daylight, and indeed,
After the ground is frozen, I should have done
Before it froze, and a gust flings a handful
Of waste leaves at my smoky lantern chimney
To make fun of my way of doing things,
Or else fun of Orion's having caught me...."

From *The Star-Splitter* by Robert Frost

* * * * *

MOON'S ENDING

Moon, worn thin to the width of a quill,
    In the dawn clouds flying,
How good to go, light into light, and still
    Giving light, dying.

By Sara Teasdale (1884–1933)

* * * * *

NEW MOON

The new moon, of no importance
lingers behind as the yellow sun glares and is gone beyond
   the sea's edge;
earth smokes blue;
the new moon, in cool height above the blushes,
brings a fresh fragrance of heaven to our senses.

By D.H. Lawrence (1885–1930)

* * * * *

"Are you cold too, poor Pleiads,
    This frosty night?"
"Yes, and so are the Hyads:
See us cuddle and hug," say the Pleiads,
"All six in a ring: it keeps us warm:
We huddle together like birds in a storm:
      It's bitter weather to-night,
      It's bitter weather to-night."

"What do you hunt, Orion,
    This starry night?"
"The Ram, the Bull and the Lion,
And the Great Bear," says Orion,
"With my starry quiver and beautiful belt
I am trying to find a good thick pelt
      To warm my shoulders to-night,
      To warm my shoulders to-night."

From *Star-Talk* by Robert Graves (1895–1985)

* * * * *

JODRELL BANK

Who were they, what lonely men
Imposed on the fact of night
The fiction of constellations
And made commensurable
The distances between
Themselves their loves and their doubt
Of governments and nations;
Who made the dark stable
When the light was not? Now
We receive the blind codes
Of spaces beyond the span
Of our myths, and a long dead star
May only echo how
There are no loves nor gods
Men can invent to explain
How lonely all men are.

By Patric Dickinson (1914–)

* * * * *

FOR THE 1956 OPPOSITION OF MARS

Red on the south horizon, brighter than
For fifteen years, the little planet glows,
And brightest yet its kindled themes impose
    On the imaginings of man.
War's omen once. Then source of fate's firm rays,
    Or, punched through the precarious sky,
    A hole on hell. And then a dry
Quantum of knowledge merely, cold in space.

Only in names from legend, history, dream,
The heart showed on its map the regions drawn:
The Horn of Ammon and the Bay of Dawn.
    Now fantasy and knowledge gleam
One red; and by the next close opposition
    Observers in the exosphere
    Should see it many times as clear,
And by the next one yet, match touch with vision,

Grasping whatever starts beneath those noons'
Blue-black intensities of sky; on sand
Blood-orange where the blue-green lowlands end;
    In thin air; under two small moons;
As spring's green flux pours down from where the
                    pole is;
    Till yellow clouds fade, while blue, higher,
    Catch the set sun with faintest fire
Over Arcadia or the Lacus Solis.

Pure joy of knowledge rides as high as art.
The whole heart cannot keep alive on either.
Wills as of Drake and Shakespeare strike together;
    Cultures turn rotten when they part.
True frontiers march with those in the mind's eye:
    The white sound rising now to fury
    In efflux from the hot venturi
As Earth's close down, gives us the endless sky.

By Robert Conquest (1917–)

* * * * *

GREENWICH OBSERVATORY

This onion-dome holds all intricacies
Of intellect and star-struck wisdom; so
Like Coleridge's head with multitudinous
Passages riddled, full of strange instruments
Unbalanced by a touch, this organism
From wires and dials spins introverted life.
It never looks, squat on its concrete shoulders
Down at the river's swarming life, nor sees
Cranes' groping insect-like activity
Nor slow procession of funnels past the docks.
Turning its inner wheels, absorbed in problems
Of space and time, it never hears
Birds singing in the park or children's laughter.
Alive, but in another way, it broods
On this its Highgate, hypnotized
In lunar reverie and calculation.
Yet night awakes it; blind lids open
Leaden to look upon the moon:

A single goggling telescopic eye
Enfolds the spheric wonder of the sky.

From *The Cruel Solstice* by Sidney Keyes (1922–1943)

* * * * *

COSMIC GEOMETRY

When the creator took his compasses
and measured out the sky from star to star,
he plotted intersecting arcs to stress
the meeting grounds where his archangels are.
In heavenly space a line does not divide;
circumference and centre coincide.

If I can think this with my finite mind,
participating in the infinite,
the universe is with my heart entwined;
I am of God a little tiny bit;
a constellation shines in every flower;
eternity imbues each mortal hour.

By Rex Raab (1914–)

* * * * *

SONG OF THE SKY LOOM

O our Mother the Earth, O our Father the Sky, . . .
Weave for us a garment of brightness;
May the warp be the white light of morning,
May the weft be the red light of evening,
May the fringes be the falling rain,
May the border be the standing rainbow.
Thus weave for us a garment of brightness,
That we may walk fittingly where birds sing,
That we may walk fittingly where grass is green,
O our Mother the Earth, O our Father the Sky.

From a North American Indian song (Tewa Tribe, Rio Grande)

* * * * *

We are the Stars which sing,
We sing with our light.
We are the birds of fire,
We fly over the sky.
Our light is a voice,
We make a road
For the spirit to pass over.

North American Indian song (from the Algonquin language)

* * * * *

Look as they rise, up rise
Over the line where sky meets the earth;
Pleiades!
Lo! They are ascending, come to guide us,
Leading us safely, keeping us one;
Pleiades,
Teach us to be, like you, united.

North American Indian (Pawnee Tribe, Nebraska)

* * * * *

I saw the new moon late yestreen,
  Wi' the auld moon in her arm;
And if ye gang to sea, maister,
  I fear we'll suffer harm.

From the anonymous Scottish ballad *Sir Patrick Spens*

* * * * *

Peep, peep,
If da wattir is ever sae deep,
A'al win ower, an' a' me sheep

(Peep, peep,
If the water is ever so deep,
I'll win over, and all my sheep.)

Anonymous guddick (riddle) from the Shetland Islands, Scotland.
The moon and stars. (They peep out in the night sky, perhaps from
behind clouds, as they pass over the sea.)

Astronomical Events

Times and dates are in Universal Time (Greenwich)
The day begins at 0 hours = midnight

NORTHERN HEMISPHERE
WINTER/SPRING ELONGATIONS OF MERCURY
IN THE WESTERN EVENING SKY
(Planet visible shortly after sunset around these dates)

February 21; June 17, 1993

February 4; May 30, 1994

January 19; May 12, 1995

January 2; April 23, 1996

April 6, 1997

March 20, 1998

March 3, 1999

February 15; June 9, 2000

January 28; May 22, 2001

January 11; May 4, 2002

April 16, 2003

March 29, 2004

March 12, 2005

SOUTHERN HEMISPHERE
WINTER/SPRING ELONGATIONS OF MERCURY
IN THE WESTERN EVENING SKY
(Planet visible shortly after sunset around these dates)

October 14, 1993

September 26, 1994

September 9, 1995

August 21; December 15, 1996

August 4; November 28, 1997

July 17; November 11, 1998

June 28; October 24, 1999

October 6, 2000

September 18, 2001

September 1; December 26, 2002

August 14; December 9, 2003

July 27; November 21, 2004

July 9; November 3, 2005

GREATEST ELONGATIONS OF VENUS
IN THE EVENING

January 19, 1993

August 24, 1994

April 1, 1996

November 6, 1997

June 11, 1999

January 17, 2001

August 22, 2002

March 29, 2004

November 3, 2005

GREATEST ELONGATIONS OF VENUS
IN THE MORNING

June 10, 1993

January 13, 1995

August 20, 1996

March 27, 1998

October 30, 1999

June 8, 2001

January 11, 2003

August 17, 2004

OPPOSITIONS OF SUPERIOR PLANETS
(at brightest periods and rising at sunset)

Mars

January 7, 1993

February 12, 1995

March 17, 1997

April 24, 1999

June 13, 2001

August 28, 2003

November 7, 2005

Jupiter

March 30, 1993

April 30, 1994

June 1, 1995

July 4, 1996

August 9, 1997

September 16, 1998

October 23, 1999

November 28, 2000

January 1, 2002

February 2, 2003

March 4, 2004

April 3, 2005

Saturn

August 19, 1993

September 1, 1994

September 14, 1995

September 26, 1996

October 10, 1997

October 23, 1998

November 6, 1999

November 19, 2000

December 3, 2001

December 17, 2002

December 31, 2003

January 13, 2005

Uranus

*(Just within naked-eye
visibility at opposition)*

July 12, 1993

July 17, 1994

July 21, 1995

July 25, 1996

July 29, 1997

August 3, 1998

August 7, 1999

August 11, 2000

August 15, 2001

August 20, 2002

August 24, 2003

August 27, 2004

September 1, 2005

TOTAL AND ANNULAR SOLAR ECLIPSES
(with regions where maximum eclipse is visible)

May 10, 1994 (Annular)—East Pacific Ocean, North America,
Atlantic Ocean, extreme NW Africa

November 3, 1994 (Total)—South America, South Atlantic Ocean

April 29, 1995 (Annular)—Pacific Ocean, South America

October 24, 1995 (Total)—Asia, Borneo, Pacific Ocean

March 9, 1997 (Total)—Siberia

February 26, 1998 (Total)—Pacific Ocean, northern South America,
Atlantic Ocean

August 22, 1998 (Annular)—Sumatra, Borneo, Pacific Ocean

February 16, 1999 (Annular)—Indian Ocean, Australia

August 11, 1999 (Total)—Atlantic Ocean, Europe, Middle East, India

June 21, 2001 (Total)—Atlantic Ocean, South Africa, Madagascar

December 14, 2001 (Annular)—Pacific Ocean, Central America

June 10, 2002 (Annular)—Pacific Ocean

December 4, 2002 (Total)—South Africa, Indian Ocean, Australia

May 31, 2003 (Annular)—Iceland

November 23, 2003 (Total)—Antarctica

April 8, 2005 (Annular/Total)—Pacific Ocean, Central America,
northern South America

October 3, 2005 (Annular)—Atlantic Ocean, Spain, Africa, Indian
Ocean

TOTAL LUNAR ECLIPSES
(with Universal Time of mid-eclipse)

December 9, 1992 (23h 44m)

June 4, 1993 (13h)

November 29, 1993 (6h 26m)

April 4, 1996 (0h 10m)

September 27, 1996 (2h 54m)

September 16, 1997 (18h 46m)

January 21, 2000 (4h 43m)

July 16, 2000 (13h 55m)

January 9, 2001 (20h 20m)

May 16, 2003 (3h 40m)

November 9, 2003 (1h 18m)

May 4, 2004 (20h 30m)

October 28, 2004 (3h 4m)

TRANSITS OF MERCURY ACROSS THE FACE OF THE SUN
(with Universal Time for Mercury being mid-way in its passage)

November 6, 1993 (3h 56m)

November 15, 1999 (21h 40m)

May 7, 2003 (7h 52m)

November 8, 2006 (21h 40m)

May 9, 2016 (14h 57m)

TRANSITS OF VENUS ACROSS THE FACE OF THE SUN
(with Universal Time for Venus being mid-way in its passage)

June 8, 2004 (8h 19m)

June 6, 2012 (1h 29m)

SOLAR SYSTEM

(Some information on remote objects or finely-graduated
calculations in the following tables is necessarily approximate
and sources can differ slightly)

SIDEREAL PERIODS

Mercury	87.97 days
Venus	224.70 "
Earth	365.26 "
Mars	686.98 "
Jupiter	11.86 years
Saturn	29.46 "
Uranus	84.01 "
Neptune	164.79 "
Pluto	247.69 "

MEAN SYNODIC PERIODS IN DAYS

Mercury	115.88
Venus	583.92
Mars	779.94
Jupiter	398.88
Saturn	378.09
Uranus	369.66
Neptune	367.49
Pluto	366.73

MEAN DISTANCES FROM THE SUN
IN ASTRONOMICAL UNITS
[1 AU = 149.6 million kilometers)

Mercury	0.387
Venus	0.723
Earth	1.000
Mars	1.524
Jupiter	5.203
Saturn	9.518
Uranus	19.176
Neptune	30.028
Pluto	39.616

INCLINATION OF ORBITS
TO THE ECLIPTIC IN DEGREES

Mercury	7.0
Venus	3.4
Earth	0.0
Moon	5.1
Mars	1.8
Jupiter	1.3
Saturn	2.5
Uranus	0.8
Neptune	1.8
Pluto	17.1

MEAN ORBITAL VELOCITIES
IN KILOMETERS PER SECOND

Mercury	47.87
Venus	35.02
Earth	29.79
Moon	1.02
Mars	24.13
Jupiter	13.06
Saturn	9.65
Uranus	6.80
Neptune	5.43
Pluto	4.74

EQUATORIAL DIAMETERS IN KILOMETERS

Sun	1392000
Moon	3476
Mercury	4878
Venus	12104
Earth	12756
Mars	6787
Jupiter	142800
Saturn	120000
Uranus	51200
Neptune	48680
Pluto	2300

SIDEREAL PERIODS OF AXIAL ROTATION

Sun	25.38 days (at its equator)
	29 days or more (at its poles)
Moon	27.322 days
Mercury	58.65 days
Venus	243.0 days (retrograde)
Earth	23.934 hours
Mars	24.623 hours
Jupiter	9.842 hours (at its equator)
Saturn	10.233 hours
Uranus	17.24 hours (retrograde)
Neptune	18.4 hours
Pluto	6.39 days (retrograde)

NUMBERS OF PLANETARY SATELLITES (MOONS)

Mercury	0
Venus	0
Earth	1
Mars	2 (Phobos and Deimos)
Jupiter	17 (4 retrograde—not the brightest ones) plus rings
Saturn	27 (1—Phoebe—retrograde) plus rings
Uranus	15 plus rings
Neptune	8 (1—Triton—retrograde plus rings)
Pluto	1 (Charon—diameter 1200 kilometers)

(Retrograde motion of a satellite here means: orbiting in the opposite direction to the axial rotation of the parent body.)

TIME

Tropical year   = 365.2422 days

Sidereal year   = 365.2564 days

Synodic month   = 29.53059 days

Sidereal month = 27.32166 days

Mean solar day = 24 hours

Sidereal day   = 23.934 hours

(For a different form of expression for some of the measurements in the tables in this Appendix—e.g., not in decimal—refer to the Glossary of Astronomical Terms in Appendix 7.)

MISCELLANEOUS

Precession of the equinoxes in longitude = 50.27 seconds of arc per year. One complete circling of the ecliptic takes about 25770 years. So the equinoxes precess one degree along the ecliptic in about 71.6 years.

Obliquity of the ecliptic (inclination of the Earth's equator to the ecliptic) = 23.43929 degrees (AD 2000)

Inclination of the Sun's equator to the ecliptic = 7.25 degrees

Inclination of the Moon's equator to the ecliptic = 1.53 degrees

Mean synodic rotation of the Sun at its equator = 27.275 days

Sun's velocity in space toward the "solar apex" (at 18h 6m + 30 deg.) in the constellation of Hercules, not far from the star Vega in adjacent Lyra = 19.75 kilometers per second

Mean distance of Earth to Moon = 384400 kilometers

One light-year = 63240 astronomical units

(In astronomy, initial capital letters are usually given to the Sun, Earth, and Moon, particularly in the context of the solar system and in the listing of planets. In literature, they are generally given lower-case initial letters).

STARS

*The 23 brightest stars (in order of decreasing brightness)
and their constellations*

Sirius (Canis Major)

Canopus (Carina)

Rigil Kentaurus (Centaurus)

Arcturus (Boötes)

Vega (Lyra)

Capella (Auriga)

Rigel (Orion)

Procyon (Canis Minor)

Achernar (Eridanus)

Betelgeuse (Orion)

Hadar (Centaurus)

Acrux (Crux—the Southern Cross)

Altair (Aquila)

Aldebaran (Taurus)

Antares (Scorpio)

Spica (Virgo)

Pollux (Gemini)

Fomalhaut (Piscis Austrinus)

Becrux (Crux—the Southern Cross)

Deneb (Cygnus)

Regulus (Leo)

Adhara (Canis Major)

Castor (Gemini)

NEAREST STARS

Of the 23 nearest star systems, only 3 are in the list above of brightest stars! They are:

Rigil Kentaurus (or Alpha Centauri)—the nearest star system to the Sun. It comprises three stars (distinguishable separately only by telescope) one of them (Proxima Centauri) being 4.2 light-years distant, the other two being 4.3 light-years distant.

Sirius—8.6 light-years (two components)

Procyon—11.4 light-years (two components)

CALENDAR NOTES

By the calendar, the 20th century ends on December 31, AD 2000. Therefore the 21st century, or the third millennium, properly begins on January 1, AD 2001. (The completion of the first year of the Christian calendar is the end of the year AD 1. This makes the end of the first decade the end of the year AD 10, the end of the first century the end of the year AD 100, etc.)

When reckoning backward in history by the calendar, the year AD 1 is followed by 1 BC. Therefore there are, for example, 3 years' difference between AD 2 and 2 BC. So, adding the first two AD years to the first two BC years results in a sum of 3 years, not 4. This must be considered in the calculation of time intervals between AD and BC. (For example, it is said that the beginning of the Indian Kali Yuga (Dark Age) occurred 5000 years before AD 1899. This places the start of Kali Yuga at 3102 BC by the calendar, for a difference of 5000 years, not 5001 years.)

The astronomer does not use the conventional calendar system of BC dating. The astronomer's system includes a year 0 so that there is an algebraic relation between the year numbers. The year 0 corresponds to the calendar's 1 BC. Years before 0 are designated as "minus" years. So, adding the first two years after 0 to the first two years before 0 results in a sum of 4 years. (For example, 5000 years before AD 1899 places the start of Kali Yuga at –3101. Sometimes this astronomer's date is incorrectly called a BC date.)

Convert a BC year to a negative year by subtracting one, and calling the year negative.

Convert a negative year to a BC year by calling the year positive and adding one.

In astronomical tables and in texts dealing with historical data, it may be found that the Julian calendar (sometimes referred to as Old Style) is used for dates after the Gregorian calendar (New Style) reform of A.D. 1582— see Gregorian calendar in the Glossary of Astronomical Terms, Appendix 7. Also, various countries changed to the Gregorian calendar at different times during the centuries following the reform. For example, Scotland changed over in 1600, but the rest of Great Britain and its North American colonies switched to the Gregorian calendar in 1752.

Conversion from the Julian calendar to the Gregorian requires the omission of ten days (i.e., adding ten days to the date) after October 4, 1582; eleven days after the end of February, 1700; twelve days after the end of February 1800; thirteen days after the end of February, 1900; and fourteen days after the end of February, 2100. The years 1600 and 2000 are by-passed in this process. For example, December 25, 1993 in the Julian calendar is the same day as January 7, 1994 in the Gregorian.

The reason for the reform was that Julius Caesar's (Julian) calendar, introduced in 45 B.C., measured the length of the year as being exactly 365.25 days, which was 11 minutes 14 seconds too long, accumulating to an error of about one day in 128 years. This shifted the seasons backward through the year, so that by the 16th century the spring equinox had drifted back to March 11.

In the Julian calendar, end-of-century years are always leap years. The Gregorian reform adds leap days in end-of-century years only when these years are divisible in whole numbers by 400—thus 1700, 1800, 1900, and 2100 are not leap years in the Gregorian calendar. Because each of these years is still a leap year by the Julian calendar, and adds an excess day, one more day has to be omitted after the end of February of these years when converting to the Gregorian calendar.

The Gregorian calendar represents a year which is only 26 seconds too long, accumulating to an error (since 1582) of one day in 3,323 years. A further correction, originally suggested by the astronomer John Herschel, would make the years 4000, 8000, 12000, and so on, ordinary years instead of leap years, thus rendering the Gregorian calendar correct to within one day in 20,000 years.

Astronomical Symbols

CONSTELLATIONS OF THE ZODIAC

Latin Name	Symbol	English Name
Aries	♈	Ram
Taurus	♉	Bull
Gemini	♊	Twins
Cancer	♋	Crab
Leo	♌	Lion
Virgo	♍	Virgin
Libra	♎	Scales
Scorpius	♏	Scorpion
Sagittarius	♐	Archer
Capricornus	♑	Goat
Aquarius	♒	Waterman
Pisces	♓	Fishes

The ecliptic actually passes through thirteen constellations. The feet of Ophiuchus (the Serpent Holder) extend between Scorpius and Sagittarius.

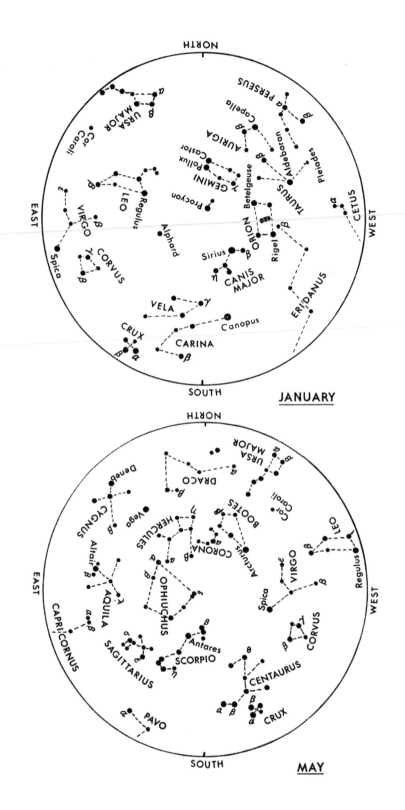

Useful Materials and Publications

12-inch diameter STUDENT CELESTIAL GLOBE (MMI Corporation, PO Box 19907, Baltimore, MD 21211, USA). Stars marked on transparent globe. Sun moveable on ecliptic. Has horizon circle.

12-inch diameter STARFINDER CELESTIAL GLOBE (Rand McNally & Company, 5535 N. Long, Chicago, IL 60630, USA). Stars marked on non-transparent globe. Has horizon circle.

THE NIGHT SKY PLANISPHERE (Sky Publishing Corporation, 49-51 Bay State Road, Cambridge, MA 02138, USA). Includes east/south/west sky view on back. Different editions for different latitudes (including Southern Hemisphere).

SKY CALENDAR (Abrams Planetarium, Michigan State University, East Lansing, MI 48824, USA). Produced monthly. Pictorial views of main sky events, with explanations.

ASTRONOMICAL CALENDAR (Astronomical Workshop, Furnam University, Greenville, SC 29613, USA). Produced annually. Excellent guide to the sky for the naked-eye observer. Fully illustrated and packed with well-researched information.

SKY & TELESCOPE (Sky Publishing Corporation, PO Box 9111, Belmont, MA 02178-9111, USA). Good monthly journal for the amateur.

Good range of technical astronomical slides from—MMI Corporation, 2950 Wyman Parkway, PO Box 19907, Baltimore, MD 21211, USA).

Computer programs for IBM PC and compatibles—VISIBLE UNIVERSE (Parsec Software, 1949 Blair Loop Road, Danville, VA 24541, USA). Outstanding program for observational astronomy and historical work. Includes horizon-elevation views and earth from space. Plots over 9000 stars and over 8000 galaxies and nebulae. SKY GLOBE (KlassM Software,284 142nd Avenue, Caledonia, MI 49316). Simple but effective on-screen celestial globe.

Planetarium systems—(MMI Corporation, PO Box 19907, 2950 Wyman Parkway, Baltimore, MD 21211, USA).

Meteorites—Two companies of several—(Bethany Trading Company, PO Box 3726-S, New Haven, CT 06525, USA. $2 catalog refundable; Robert A. Haag Meteorites, 2990 East Michigan Street, PO Box 27527, Tucson, AZ 85726, USA. $5 catalog refundable.)

Dark glass often used for observing eclipses and sunspots—Number 14 (USA) arc-welder's glass, available from welding supply shops. This glass is supplied along with welding goggles retailed by Amateur Astronomers, Inc., PO Box 761, Woodbridge, NJ 07095, USA.

SKYLINE—astronomy news and information telephone number in USA (a Sky Publishing service)—617-497-4168.

BOOKS OF INTEREST

Wide range of serious astronomical books from—(Willmann-Bell, Inc., PO Box 35025, Richmond, VA 23235, USA).

Astronomers—Biographical Dictionary of Scientists series— (Peter Bedrick Books, New York).

The Astronomers by Colin Ronan (Evans Brothers, London).

Astronomy and the Imagination by Norman Davidson (Arkana/Penguin Books). Companion volume to *Sky Phenomena.*

Copernicus by Angus Armitage (Thomas Yoseloff, London & New York).

A History of Astronomy from Thales to Kepler by J. L. E. Dreyer (Dover, New York).

John Kepler by Angus Armitage (Faber & Faber, London).

Movement and Rhythms of the Stars by Joachim Schultz (Floris Books & Anthroposophic Press, New York).

The New Patterns in the Sky—Myths and Legends of the Stars by Julius Staal (McDonald & Woodward, Blacksburg, Virginia, USA).

Sidereus Nuncius or the Sidereal Messenger by Galileo Galilei (University of Chicago Press, Chicago & London). Galileo documents his early telescopic discoveries.

The Sleepwalkers—A History of Man's Changing Vision of the Universe by Arthur Koestler (Penguin Books, UK). Contains much fascinating detail on the lives and works of Copernicus, Brahe, and Kepler.

Star Tales by Ian Ridpath (Universe Books, New York). Mythology of the constellations with reproductions of engravings from Johann Bode's *Uranographia* (1801) and John Flamsteed's *Atlas Coelestis* (1729).

They Dance in the Sky—Native American Star Myths by Jean Monroe & Ray Williamson (Houghton Mifflin, Boston).

Theories of the World from Antiquity to the Copernican Revolution by Michael Crowe (Dover, New York).

The World of Copernicus by Angus Armitage (Mentor Books, USA).

STAR ATLASES

Will Tirion's Bright Star Atlas (Willmann-Bell, PO Box 35025, Richmond, VA 23235, USA). Includes horizon views. High standard.

Norton's 2000.0 Star Atlas and Reference Handbook (Longman Scientific & Technical, UK; John Wiley, New York). The amateur astronomer's classic.

LITERATURE ON ASTRONOMICAL ORGANIZATIONS, RESOURCES, ETC.

UNITED STATES—Sky & Telescope's *Astronomical Directory* supplement (Sky Publishing Corporation, 49 Bay State Road, Cambridge, MA 02138).

UNITED KINGDOM—Federation of Astronomical Societies publishes a *Handbook for Astronomical Societies* (Brian Jones, Editor, 17 Havelock Street, Thornton, Bradford, West Yorkshire, BD13 3HA).

WORLD—*International Directory of Astronomical Associations and Societies* (Dr A. Heck, Observatoir Astronomique, 11 rue de l' Universite, F-67000 Strasbourg, France).

Some Famous Individuals in the History of Astronomy

Thales (circa 624–547 BC) Greek

Pythagoras (flourished 6th century BC) Greek

Plato (circa 427–347 BC) Greek

Aristotle (384–322 BC) Greek

Aristarchus of Samos (flourished 280–264 BC) Greek

Eratosthenes (circa 276–196 BC) Greek

Hipparchus (flourished 146–127 BC) Greek

Ptolemy—Claudius Ptolemaeus —(circa AD 90–168) Greek

Nicolaus Copernicus (1473–1543) Polish

Tycho Brahe (1546–1601) Danish

Galileo—Galileo Galilei—(1564–1642) Italian

Johannes Kepler (1571–1630) German

Johann Bayer (1572–1625) German

Christiaan Huygens (1629–1695) Dutch

Isaac Newton (1642–1727) English

Edmond Halley (1656–1742) English

James Bradley (1693–1762) English

Charles Messier (1730–1817) French

William Herschel (1738–1822) German–English

Giuseppe Piazzi (1746–1826) Italian

Johann Bode (1747–1826) German

Pierre Laplace (1749–1827) French

Friedrich Bessel (1784–1846) German

Urbain Le Verrier (1811–1877) French

Johann Galle (1812–1910) German

John Couch Adams (1819–1892) English

Giovanni Schiaparelli (1835–1910) Italian

Percival Lowell (1855–1916) American

Albert Einstein (1879–1955) German–American

Edwin Hubble (1889–1953) American

Jan Hendrik Oort (1900–1992) Dutch

Clyde Tombaugh (born 1906) American

Glossary of
Astronomical Terms

airglow—The faint, ever-present glow in the Earth's atmosphere. Often called 'nightglow.'

albedo—The light-reflecting power of a non-luminous object, such as a planet or a moon.

alpha—The first letter of the Greek alphabet, used in star naming and usually indicating the brightest star in a constellation.

altitude—The angular distance of an object above or below the horizon measured in degrees (0-90) on a circle which is vertical to the horizon and passing through the zenith and nadir. A position above the horizon has a "plus" value and one below a "minus" value.

aphelion—The point in the orbit of an object round the Sun when it is farthest from the Sun. Opposite point to perihelion.

apogee—The point in the orbit of an object round the Earth when it is farthest from the Earth. Opposite point to perigee.

apparition—The period during which a planet, star, etc., can be observed.

appulse—The apparent close approach of one celestial body to another.

apsides—The two points on an elliptical orbit which lie on its major (longest) axis and where the curvature is greatest.

arc second—An angle of 1/3600 of a degree or 1/60 of an arc minute.

ashen light—The faint glow said to be occasionally observed on the unlit area of Venus in crescent phase. See also earthshine.

astronomical unit—The mean distance between the Earth and the Sun (149.6 million kilometers).

azimuth—The angular distance measured in degrees (0-360) along the horizon from the north point through east, south, and west. Sometimes it is measured from the south point, but in the same direction.

blue moon—Not an astronomical term, but worth mentioning. Unusual atmospheric conditions can cause the Moon to appear blue, as when this was photographed during a 1984 eruption of Mauna Loa volcano in Hawaii. The Moon also turned blue on September 26, 1950, in connection with forest fires in Canada. Such occurrences in earlier times may have led to the term "once in a blue moon" meaning a rare event. A blue moon now commonly means two full moons falling within a calendar month—which happens on average every 2.72 years. About one year in 19 has two blue moons.

celestial equator—The great circle produced by the intersection of the Earth's equatorial plane with the celestial sphere.

celestial latitude—Angular measurement in degrees (0—90) north or south of the ecliptic. Northwards has a "plus" value, southwards a "minus".

celestial longitude—Angular measurement in degrees (0—360) from the vernal equinox point (first point of Aries) eastwards along the ecliptic.

celestial poles—The two points at which the extension of the Earth's axis of rotation meets the celestial sphere.

colures—The two great circles passing through the celestial poles and intersecting the ecliptic at either the equinoxes or the solstices.

conjunction—The situation when celestial bodies have either the same celestial longitude or the same right ascension.

culmination—The passage of a celestial body across the observer's meridian. Upper culmination is the passage nearest to the observer's zenith, lower culmination the one farthest from the zenith. Only circumpolar stars can be seen at both culminations (when the body is observed turning round the pole). Culmination is also used as a general term for the moment when a celestial body reaches its greatest altitude above the horizon (upper culmination).

day—1. Apparent solar day: the interval between two successive transits of the observed Sun across the meridian. Not a constant unit of time. 2. Mean solar day: the interval of 24 hours between two successive transits of the mean Sun across the meridian. The mean Sun moves at a constant speed in an imaginary circular orbit round the celestial equator in a year and its movement is measured in right ascension. 3. Sidereal day: the period of the Earth's rotation on its axis measured in relation to the stars. 23 hours 56 minutes 4 seconds.

declination (Dec.)—Angular measurement in degrees (0—90) north or south of the celestial equator. Northward has a "plus" value and southward a "minus."

dichotomy—The exact half-phase of the Moon, Mercury, or Venus.

direct motion—1. Movement of a planet, etc., from west to east against the background of stars. The orbits of all planets in the solar system have direct motion—i.e., anticlockwise as seen from the north pole of the ecliptic. Compare: retrograde motion. 2. Anticlockwise rotation of a planet on its axis as seen from the north pole of the ecliptic.

diurnal motion—The apparent daily motion of celestial bodies across the sky from east to west.

earthshine—Also called ashen light. Sunlight reflected from the Earth and illuminating the night side of the Moon when it is at or near crescent phase.

eccentricity—A measure of how much the elliptical orbit of a planet, etc., deviates from circularity. Of the naked-eye planets, Mercury has the greatest eccentricity and Venus the least. Pluto, beyond the naked eye, has the greatest eccentricity of all. For a circular orbit, eccentricity = 0. The Earth has an eccentricity of 0.016722, which is at present very slowly decreasing toward circularity over thousands of years.

ecliptic—The apparent path of the Sun, in a great circle against the stars, in one year.

ecliptic poles—The two points on the celestial sphere lying 90 degrees north or south of the ecliptic. The north ecliptic pole is in the constellation of Draco at right ascension 18 hours, declination +66.5 degrees. The south ecliptic pole is in the constellation of Dorado at right ascension 6 hours, declination -66.5 degrees. They are 23.5 degrees from the celestial poles, which expresses the obliquity of the ecliptic.

elongation—The angular distance between the Sun and a planet or the Moon, or between a planet and its satellite. Measured along the ecliptic in degrees.

epoch—The date and time on which the coordinates for particular calculations of position are based. Currently the standard epoch is the beginning of a Julian year at 12 hours on January 1, AD 2000 at Greenwich (also written as "J2000.0").

equation of time—The difference in time between the mean position of the Sun and its true position. Used to adjust sundial time to clock time.

equinoxes—The two points on the celestial sphere at which the celestial equator and the ecliptic intersect. At the beginning of spring (in the Northern Hemisphere) the Sun stands on what is technically termed the dynamical equinox—also called the vernal equinox—and popularly referred to as the spring equinox. This is also the first point of Aries. On reaching this point the Sun passes from south to north of the celestial equator. At the autumnal equinox (for the Northern Hemisphere) the Sun passes from north to south of the equator.

fundamental stars—Stars whose positions and proper motions are known so accurately that the positions of other stars can be determined from them.

Galaxy—When written with an initial capital letter, the spiral system of stars to which the sun belongs. Also called the Milky Way Galaxy. All the visible stars in the sky belong to it.

geocentric—Earth-centered.

great circle—A circle on the surface of a sphere which has its center at the center of the sphere. It is thus the largest type of circle on the sphere and divides it into two equal parts.

Gregorian calendar—The calendar used throughout most of the world today and originally decreed for Roman Catholic countries by Pope Gregory XIII in 1582. Until then the Julian calendar (introduced by Julius Caesar in 45 B.C.) had allowed the moment of spring equinox to slip back to March 11. The Gregorian calendar adjusted the future calculation of leap years and erased 10 days from the calendar of 1582 without breaking the sequence of named days of the week. Thursday, October 4 was proclaimed to be followed by Friday, October 15.

heliocentric—Sun-centered.

horizon—The astronomical horizon is the great circle in which the celestial sphere is intersected by a plane through the observer's position and at right angles to a line between the observer and his or her zenith.

hour circles—Great circles on the celestial sphere which pass through the celestial poles and along which declination is measured.

inner planets—See terrestrial planets.

inferior planets—Those whose orbits lie between Sun and Earth (i.e., Mercury and Venus). Originally indicated the planets which lay "below" the Sun in the geocentric system.

Julian calendar—See Gregorian calendar.

Julian date—The number of days and decimal points of a day, calculated from noon to noon at Greenwich, that have elapsed since January 1, 4713 B.C. This is expressed as the Julian day number of a Julian year. The system makes one day exactly 24 hours and one year exactly 365.25 days and is used by the astronomer to calculate over long periods. For example, 6 p.m. on March 1, 2000, is day number 2451605.25. The system was pioneered in 1582 by the French scholar Joseph Scaliger and named after his father Julius Caesar Scaliger.

libration—Geometrical librations are apparent rocking motions of the Moon as seen from Earth, due to the Moon's elliptical orbit and the orbit's inclination to the ecliptic. These and other, smaller libration effects result in more of the Moon's globe being visible from Earth than would otherwise be possible. Over a 30-year period, libration allows 59 percent of the Moon's surface to be visible from Earth.

light-year—The distance which it is understood light travels in space over a period of one tropical year; 63240 astronomical units.

limb—The apparent edge of a celestial body with a detectable disk, such as the Sun, Moon, or a planet.

lunation—A synodic month. See month.

lunar year—Twelve moon cycles, or months, amounting to about 354 days, and used in the Islamic calendar. This means that the beginning of the lunar year steps backward through the seasons in intervals of about 11 days and passes through all of them in about 33 years. The lunar month (and day and year) of this calendar begins at sunset and is based on the sighting of the first crescent moon. The Jewish calendar also uses such a lunar month but keeps the year in step with the seasons by inserting a thirteenth month every three years or so.

magnitude—1. Apparent magnitude: the degree of brightness of a star or planet as determined from the Earth by the human eye (visual magnitude) or by using photography or photometry for the same or a similar purpose. 2. Absolute magnitude: the apparent magnitude that a star would have if it were observed from a distance of 32.6 light years. (Brightness is classified in such a way that as brightness increases the magnitude number decreases. Therefore, stars with "minus" magnitudes are brighter than those with "plus" magnitudes. For example—in apparent magnitude, Vega is 0.0, the brighter Sirius is -1.5, and the fainter Regulus is 1.3.)

meridian—Celestial meridian: the great circle which passes through the north and south celestial poles and the observer's zenith, and intersects the observer's horizon at the due north and south points.

month— 1. Synodic month (lunation): the interval between two successive new moons. 29 days 12 hours 44 minutes 2.9 seconds. 2. Sidereal month: the period taken by the Moon to make one complete circuit of the celestial sphere in relation to the stars. 27 days 7 hours 43 minutes 11 seconds.

nadir—The point opposite the observer's zenith on the celestial sphere, i.e., directly beneath the observer. See zenith.

nebula—A cloud of gas and dust within the Milky Way Galaxy. Nebulae can be observed as either luminous patches of light or as dark shapes against brighter backgrounds. The term "nebulae" was originally applied to galaxies and star clusters too.

nodes—The two crossing points on the celestial sphere of a celestial body's orbit with, usually, the ecliptic. When the body, say the Moon or a planet, crosses the ecliptic from south to north it is at the ascending node, and when it crosses from north to south it is at the descending node. The nodes move along the ecliptic and when the movement is in the same direction as the orbiting of the body it is called the progression of the nodes. Movement in the opposite direction is the regression of the nodes. The Moon's nodes regress westward all the way round the ecliptic in 18.61 years.

nutation—Means nodding. A slight undulation in the precessional movement of the celestial poles round the poles of the ecliptic. Mainly due to the influence of the Moon which causes one wave of the undulation to take place in 18.6 years and divert the poles by about 9 seconds of arc from a mean circle of movement. Named and discovered by James Bradley in England who traced it during one cycle of the Moon's nodes between 1727 and 1748.

obliquity of the ecliptic—The angle at which the ecliptic is inclined to the celestial equator. This angle very slowly fluctuates (decreases at this point in history) and in January 2000 will be 23 degrees 26 minutes 21 seconds.

occultation—When a celestial body is observed to pass in front of an apparently smaller one, partly or completely obscuring it. Stars and planets are frequently occulted by the Moon.

opposition—When the Moon or a superior planet stands opposite, or 180 degrees from, the Sun as seen from Earth. A planet in opposition rises at sunset and sets at sunrise.

outer planets—Those whose orbits lie outside the asteroid belt. Jupiter, Saturn, Uranus, Neptune, and Pluto.

parallax—1. Annual parallax: the apparent shift in position of a celestial body that results from the change in the observer's position during the Earth's yearly orbit round the Sun. 2. Diurnal parallax: the apparent shift in position of a celestial body resulting from the change in position of the observer as the Earth rotates on its axis.

perigee—The point in the orbit of an object round the Earth when it is nearest to the Earth. The Moon's perigee makes one revolution against the stars eastward in 8.85 years.

perihelion—The point in the elliptical orbit of an object round the Sun when it is nearest to the Sun. Perihelia have very slow movements and when this is in the same direction as the orbiting of the body it is called the advance of perihelion. The Earth's perihelion advances gradually eastward in the opposite direction to precession and makes one revolution from vernal equinox to vernal equinox in about 21000 years. This means that the date on which the Earth is at perihelion gradually falls later in the year—discounting short-term inequalities in the lengths of calendar years. Currently the Earth is at perihelion, or closest to the Sun, around January 3.

phase angle—The angle between a line connecting an object to the Sun and a line connecting the object to the Earth. The object can be the Moon or one of the planets. This angle determines how much of the Moon or planet is seen to be illuminated from Earth (phase). The Moon and inferior planets go through phases from new to full, but the superior planets can never be seen as crescent and always remain gibbous. The least phase of the superior planets takes place at quadrature when the phase angle is greatest. Mars at quadrature is like the Moon three or four days from full.

precession of the equinoxes—The gradual westward movement of the vernal and autumnal equinoxes along the ecliptic. Caused by the identical precession of the Earth's axis which makes the north celestial pole describe a circular movement among the stars round the north pole of the ecliptic. A corresponding movement is made by the south celestial pole round the south pole of the ecliptic. One complete rotation takes about 25770 years (25920 is an idealized figure, rounding off to 72 years the period in which the equinoxes move one degree). Around 3000 BC the vernal equinox lay beside the star Aldebaran in Taurus. Now it is in Pisces, just south of the Square of Pegasus. (In early astronomy the term for "westward" was "in precedence", or toward the celestial bodies which preceded in the diurnal turning of the sky. Precession was part of Copernicus's third motion of the Earth and he referred to the motion as going "westward, i.e., turning in precedence".)

proper motion—The apparent angular motion per year of a star on the celestial sphere. This is an individual type of motion and over thousands of years causes the shapes of constellations to change. It was first detected by Edmond Halley in 1718.

quadrature—When the Moon or a planet is 90 degrees from the Sun as seen from Earth.

refraction—Atmospheric refraction: the slight apparent displacement of celestial objects upward toward the zenith as their light is refracted by the Earth's atmosphere. At the horizon, displacement can amount to just over half a degree, so that the Sun or Moon can appear to be on the horizon but are "technically" below it.

retardation—The difference between the time of moonrise on two successive nights.

retrograde motion—1. The apparent east to west motion of a planet, etc., against the background of the stars. For example, superior planets are seen to retrograde when passing through opposition. 2. Clockwise rotation of a planet on its axis as seen from the north pole of the ecliptic.

right ascension (R.A.)—Angular measurement, generally expressed in hours, minutes, and seconds, from the vernal equinox point (first point of Aries) eastward along the celestial equator. One hour equals 15 degrees of arc and four minutes equal one degree of arc.

risings and settings—1. Acronical (related to the night) rising or setting is when a star or planet rises or sets at sunset. 2. Cosmic (related to the day) rising or setting is when a star or planet rises or sets at sunrise. (Precise acronical and cosmic events are not normally visible to the naked eye. One can, however, speak of "apparent" acronical rising and "apparent" cosmic setting which are, respectively, the first visible rising at dusk and the last visible setting at dawn.) 3. Heliacal (related to the sun) rising or setting is when a star or planet visibly rises a little before sunrise, or visibly sets a little after sunset.

shadow bands—Elongated patterns of light and shadow which are briefly observed moving rapidly over light surfaces shortly before and after totality in a solar eclipse.

solar apex—The point on the celestial sphere toward which the Sun (and the planets along with it) is currently moving relative to other stars in the vicinity. This point lies on the sphere near the star Vega (and in the adjacent constellation of Hercules) at a position of right ascension 18 hours 6 minutes, declination +30 degrees (epoch 1950). The velocity at which the Sun is moving is calculated at 19.75 kilometers a second. The solar antapex, the point from which the Sun is receding, lies in the opposite direction in the constellation of Columba.

solstices—The two points on the ecliptic which are mid-way between the equinoxes and at the greatest angular distances north and south of the celestial equator. The northern-most point is the summer solstice and the southern-most the winter solstice (for the Northern Hemisphere)—the seasons being the opposite in the Southern Hemisphere when the Sun is at these points.

stationary points—Where a planet seen from Earth is between direct and retrograde motion and is stationary with respect to the stars.

sunspot cycle—The average period of 11 years in which sunspot activity returns to a maximum. The recurrence of maximum has been known to fluctuate between eight years and fifteen years.

superior planets—Those whose orbits lie outside that of the Earth (i.e., Mars, Jupiter, Saturn, and so on). Originally indicated the planets which lay "above" the Sun in the geocentric system.

synodic period—The cycle of a planet in relation to the Sun, as seen from Earth. The average period between two successive conjunctions of the planet with the Sun.

syzygy—Conjunction or opposition of the Moon or a planet to the the Sun.

terminator—The boundary between the sunlit and the dark areas on the surface of the Moon or a planet where sunrise or sunset take place.

terrestrial planets—Those whose orbits lie within the asteroid belt (i.e., Mercury, Venus, Earth, and Mars). Also referred to as inner planets.

transit—1. The passage of Mercury or Venus across the face of the Sun. 2. The passage of a planet's satellite or its shadow across the face of the planet. 3. The passage, closest to the observer's zenith, of a celestial body (e.g., the Sun) across the observer's meridian—also called upper culmination.

twilight—1. Civil twilight: ends in the evening and begins in the morning when the center of the Sun is 6 degrees below the horizon. The ending of civil twilight in the evening indicates when artificial lighting is needed and for navigation it is usually described as being when the brightest stars become visible. 2. Nautical twilight: ends in the evening and begins in the morning when the center of the Sun is 12 degrees below the horizon. At the end of nautical twilight in the evening the sea horizon is generally no longer visible. 3. Astronomical twilight: ends in the evening and begins in the morning when the center of the Sun is 18 degrees below the horizon. At the end of astronomical twilight in the evening, 6th magnitude stars (around the limit for detection with the naked eye) are just visible at the zenith in a clear sky.

Universal Time (UT)—The measure of time in general use. The mean solar time at the meridian of Greenwich, England. The day begins at midnight.

year—1. Tropical year: the seasonal year. The time taken by the Sun to complete one circuit round the celestial sphere, from vernal equinox to vernal equinox. 365 days 5 hours 48 minutes 45 seconds. 2. Sidereal year: the time taken by the Sun to complete one circuit round the celestial sphere in relation to the stars. Also, the time taken by the Earth to complete one orbit of the Sun in relation to the stars. 365 days 6 hours 9 minutes 8.4 seconds. (The difference of about 20 minutes between the sidereal year and the tropical year is the effect of the precession of the equinoxes.)

zenith—The point on the celestial sphere vertically above the observer, on a line at right angles to the observer's horizon plane.

zodiac—A band round the celestial sphere, extending about 9 degrees on either side of the ecliptic. The Sun, Moon and planets out to Neptune make their movements entirely within it. The sidereal zodiac consists of twelve patterns of stars (or zodiacal constellations) round the band, named from antiquity as Aries, Taurus, etc. This zodiac is distinct from the tropical zodiac which has the same twelve traditional names for its divisions of the band, but is differently placed. The tropical zodiac rotates through the sidereal zodiac with precession, as its first point (of Aries) is the vernal equinox. This first point of Aries today stands almost at the beginning (western boundary) of the star constellation of Pisces. The twelve divisions of the tropical zodiac, called signs, are equal in length and this zodiac was traditionally used by astrologers. The vernal equinox is gradually moving westwards out of Pisces and is approaching the constellation of Aquarius. This is connected with the approach of the so-called Age of Aquarius—though one has to distinguish between literature which places the start of this period at the equinox's entry into the constellation, or near its arrival at the middle of the constellation, in addition to deciding where the boundaries of the zodiacal constellations are (e.g., if the Zodiacal Ages are equal in length, then the constellations must also be equal). The modern astronomer conventionally divides the zodiac into unequal lengths.

A

Aboriginals, Australian, 105, 108
Achernar (star), 107
Akkadians,(Semitic people), 19
Aldebaran (star), 17, 68
Algol (star), 7
Algonquin poetry, 159
Alkaid (star), 3
Allen, Richard, 105
Almagest (Ptolemy), 78
Alpha Centauri (star), 108
Alpha Pavonis (star), 107
Altitude measurements of celestial
    objects, 37-38
Amasis II (King), 38
American Astronomical Society, xii
*Anatomie of the World: The First
    Anniversary* (Donne)—poem,
    130-131
*Anleitung zur Kenntniss des
    gestirnten Himmels* (Bode), 83
Annual parallax, 70-71
Antarctic Circle, 27, 40
Antares (star), 19
Apian, Peter, 92
Appointment, The (Prudhomme)—
    poem, 148
A Private Universe, xi
Aquarius (Waterman) constellation,
    20, 93
Aquinas, Thomas, 55
Arabs
    constellation/star naming and
        the, 7, 8, 17, 19
    Eridanus constellation and the,
        107
    Pole Star and the, 6
Archer (Sagittarius) constellation,
    14, 20, 111
Arctic Circle, 27, 40
Arcturus (star), 79
Argo constellation, 106-107
Aries (Ram) constellation, 17
Aristarchus (moon crater), 47
Aristarchus of Samos, 69
Aristotle, 55, 70
Association for Astronomy
    Education, xii
Assyrian people, 7, 19
Asterism, 2. *See also specific asterism*
Asteroids, 84
Astronomer, The (Mackay)—poem,
    144-145

Astronomers, famous, 182
Astronomical Calender (Ottewell),
    xiv
Astronomical Society of the Pacific,
    xi-xii
Astronomica (Manilus)—poem, 123
Astronomy and the Imagination
    (Davidson), xii, 14n
At a Lunar Eclipse (Hardy)—poem,
    149
Augustine (Saint), 55
Auriga (Charioteer) constellation, 7

B

Babylonians, 20, 120-121
Ballad of the Northern Lights, The
    (Service)—poem, 153
Bayer, Johann, 6, 107
Berossos (Babylonian priest), 17
Bessel, Friedrich, 71
Bhadrabahu (astronomer), 92
Bhattotpala (astronomer), 92
Big Dipper, 2-3, 6, 11
Bode's Law, 82-85
Bohemia, Lyra constellation and, 8
Book of the Dead, 120n
Bradley, James, 70
Brahe, Tycho, 8, 70-73, 89-91
Britons, Lyra constellation and, 8
Bull (Taurus) constellation, 17, 111
Bushmen, South African, 108

C

Calendar month, 44
Calendar notes, 173-174
Canadian Astronomical Society, xii
Cancer (Crab) constellation, 18
Canon's Yeoman's Tale (Chaucer)—
    poem, 125
Canopus (star), 107
Canterbury Tales (Chaucer)—poem,
    126
Cape Clouds (galaxies), 107
Capella (star), 7
Capricornus (Goat) constellation, 20
Carina constellation, 106, 107
Cassiopeia constellation, 7-8
Castor (star), 18
Celestial equator
    celestial sphere construction
        and, 13

Earth's equator and, 27
horizontal movements and, 26
Southern Hemisphere and, 102, 108-110
zodiacal constellations and, 14-15
Celestial sphere effect, 1-2, 13-16, 102-103
Centaur constellation, 107-108
Ceres (asteroid), 83, 84
Chaldeans, Crab constellation and, 18
Charioteer (Auriga) constellation, 7
Childe Harold's Pilgrimage (Byron)—poem, 140
Chinese
    Canopus (star) and the, 107
    comets and the, 89, 92
    meteor showers and the, 95
    Pole Star and the, 6
    Scales constellation and the, 19
Choose Something Like a Star (Frost)—poem, 154
Chronometer, 33
Circumference of Earth, measuring, 29
Circumpolar stars, 1-5, 9-10
Coal Sack (gas cloud), 105
Columbus, Christopher, 54-56
Coma of comets, 88
Comets
    conic curves and, 92, 97-100
    distance from Earth of, 90-91
    mystery of, 88-89
    predicting return of, 91-92
Conic curves, 41, 92-93, 97-100
Constellations, 6-9. *See also specific constellation;* Zodiacal constellations
Consummation (Traherne)—poem, 136
Contemplation de la Nature (Bonnet), 82
Cook, James, 33
Copernicus, Nicolaus, 67-71, 74, 78
Corsali, Andrea, 103, 104
Cosmic Geometry (Raab)—poem, 158
Cosmic Man—poem, 117-118
Cosmographia (Silvestris)—poem, 122n
Crab (Cancer) constellation, 18
Crux constellation, 103-106, 108
Cuneiform texts, Archer constellation and, 20
Cygnus (Swan) constellation, 8

D

d'Acosta, Cristoval, 103
Dante (poet), 55, 104-105
Date Line, 31-32
Dead Man Ariseth and Singeth a Hymn to the Sun, The—hymn, 119-120

Democritus Platonissans (More)—poem, 135
Deneb (star), 8, 9
Diameters of planets, 169
Diamond Cross (asterism), 105-106
Discarded Image (Lewis), xi
Diurnal parallax, 90-91
Doctor Faustus (Marlowe)—poem, 126-127
Donne, John, 66
Dorado constellation, 114
Dragon (Draco) constellation, 9
Dubhe (star), 3
Duhalde, Oscar, 113-115

E

Earth
    circumference of, measuring the, 29
    comet distances from, 90-91
    Copernicus and the, 67-71, 74, 78
    Kepler and the, 73-77
    modern astronomy and the, 79-80
    motionless concept of, 66-67, 78
    observation of from Moon, 49-50
    spherical nature of the, 55-56
Eclipses, 54-59, 165-166
Educational supports for astronomy, xi-xiii
Egypt
    Argo constellation and, 106
    Book of the Dead and, 120n
    Dragon constellation and, 9
    Virgin constellation and, 19
Elliptical orbits
    envelope of lines and, 82
    geometrical picture of solar system and, 77
    inclinations of, 168
    Kepler and, 74
    music of the spheres and, 76
Emerson, Ralph Waldo, 143
Encke, Johann, 91
Epicycle, planet movements and the, 74, 78, 80-81
Equator, 27. *See also* Celestial equator
Eratosthenes (astronomer), 20, 29, 106, 107
Eridanus (the river) constellation, 107
Eta Aquarids meteor shower, 93
Euphrates civilization, Scorpion constellation and, 19

F

False Cross (asterism), 105-106
Faust (Goethe)—poem, 138
Filters, viewing the Sun and, 57
Finnish people, 6
Fireballs, 96

Fishes (Pisces) constellation, 14, 20
Fomalhaut (star), 20
For the 1956 Opposition of Mars (Conquest)—poem, 156-157
Frederick II (King), 70
Froude, James, 105
Full Moon (de la Mare)—poem, 153

G

Galileo, 71
Geminids meteor showers, 96
Gemini (Twins) constellation, 14, 18, 111, 115
Geometrical symmetry between Northern and Southern Hemispheres, 115-116
Gnomon, xii
Gnomon, vertical, 38
Goat (Capricornus) constellation, 20
Golden Fleece legend, 17
Great Bear (Ursa Major) constellation, 2, 6-7, 116
Greeks
    Argo constellation and the, 106
    comets and the, 89
    constellation naming and the, 7-8, 9
    Earth movements and the, 69
    Eridanus constellation and the, 107
    zodiacal constellations and the, 17-20
Greenwich (London) time, 33, 34
Greenwich Observatory (Keyes)—poem, 157-158
Guddick (riddle), 159

H

Habington, William, 133
Hadar (star), 108
Half Moon Shows a Face of Plaintive Sweetness, The (Rossetti)—poem, 148
Halley, Edmond, 79, 91
Halley's comet, 91-92, 93
Hamal (star), 17
Harmonices Mundi (Kepler), 86
Harrison, John, 33
Harvest Moon, 48
Harvard-Smithsonian Center for Astrophysics, xi
Hebrew people, 19, 20
Hercules constellation, 80
Herodotus (historian), 101, 102
Herschel, William, 47, 83
Hevelius, Johannes, 17
Hillyer, Robert, 120n
Hipparchus (astronomer), 107
History (Herodotus), 101
Humboldt, Alexander von, 104

Hymn (Addison), 137
Hymn on the Morning of Christ's Nativity (Milton), 132-133
Hymn to the North Star (Bryant), 142

I

India
    Archer constellation and, 20
    Canopus (star) and, 107
    comet predictions and, 92
    Lion constellation and, 18
    Pole Star and, 6-7
    Virgin constellation and, 19
Inferior planets, 60
International Astronomical Union, 114
International Planetarium Society, xii
Invocation—poem, 120-121
Isabella (Queen), 55

J

Jewish people, 20-21
Jodrell Bank (Dickinson)—poem, 156
Journal of the British Astronomical Association, 5n
Julius Caesar (Shakespeare)—poem, 128-129
Juno (asteroid), 84
Jupiter, 64, 66, 68, 77

K

Kepler, Johannes, 73-77, 85-87, 131-132
Kepler's Geometrical Cosmology (Field), 87

L

Lappish people, 6
Latin literature, Great Bear constellation and, 7
Latitude measurements, 32, 33
Leo (Lion) constellation, 18
Leonid meteor showers, 94
Libra (Scales) constellation, 19
Lion (Leo) constellation, 18
Literature and the Moon, 46-47.
    See also Poetry, hymns, and the stars
Locksley Hall (Tennyson)—poem, 144
Lodestar (guiding star), 6
Longfellow, Henry W., 104-105
Longitude measurements, 32-34
Luther, Martin, 70
Lyra constellation, 8

M

Macbeth (Shakespeare), 47
Magellan, Ferdinand, 30, 31, 107
Magellanic Clouds (galaxies), Large/Small, 107, 113
Magellan's Spot, 105
Man (Herbert)—poem, 132
Man of Lawes Tale, The (Chaucer)—poem, 125
Mapping/graphing stars, 3-5
   equator and, Earth's, 177-178
   freehand alternative when, 21-22
   Southern Hemisphere and, 109-111
   zodiacal constellations and, 15-16
Mars
   Earth-centered system and, 67
   elliptical orbit of, 77
   Platonic solids theory and, 86
   Sun movements and visibility of, 64
   synodic period and, 65
Martyr, Peter, 105
Materials and publications, useful, 179-181
Mayan people, 19
Mechain, Pierre, 91
Meditation Under Stars (Meredith)—poem, 146
Meeus, Jean, 5n
Merak (star), 3
Mercury
   Earth-centered system and, 66, 67
   elliptical orbit of, 77
   orbits around Sun by, 68
   Platonic solids theory and, 86
   Sun movements and visibility of, 60-63
   transits across the Sun by, 166
   winter/spring elongations of, 161-162
Meteorites, 96
Meteors, 93-96
Meteorologia (Aristotle), 89
Mistress of Vision, The (Thompson)—poem, 151
Months' relationship to the Moon, 44
Moon
   arc movements of the, 45
   Brahe and the, 72
   calendar showing phases of the, 51
   diurnal parallax measurements and the, 90-91
   Earth-centered system and the, 66, 67
   eclipses of the, 54-55, 57-59, 166
   horizontal motion of the, 26
   literature and the, 46-47
   observing Earth from the, 49-50
   phases of the, 42-44, 52-53
   Southern Hemisphere and the, 111-112

tides and the, 48-49
Moons, number of planetary, 170
Moon's Ending (Teasdale)—poem, 155
Music and celestial movements, 76
Mysterium Cosmographicum (Kepler), 85, 86-87, 131
Mythology and constellations, 6-9, 17-21, 106

N

Neco (King), 101
Neptune, 68, 84, 85
New Moon, The (Bryant)—poem, 142
New Moon (Lawrence)—poem, 155
Night (Blake)—poem, 139
Night Thoughts (Young)—poem, 137
Nocturnal (time device), 9-11
Noon, determination of local, 28-29, 33
North celestial pole
   celestial sphere and, 1
   mapping stars and, 3
   movement of the, 5, 9, 14
   navigation by the, 6-7
Northern Cross asterism, 8
Northern Hemisphere, 2-5. See also specific subject areas within
   borderline zones in, 27-28
   geometrical symmetry between Southern and, 115-116
   winter/spring elongations of Mercury in, 161
North pole, 25, 26
Nox nocti indicat Scientiam. DAVID (Habington)—poem, 133
Nucleus of comets, 88

O

Occultation of stars, 47
Ode to Heaven (Shelley)—-poem, 141
Olbers, Heinrich, 83
On the Revolutions of the Heavenly Spheres (Copernicus), 69
Oppositions of superior planets, 163-165
Orionids meteor shower, 93, 96
Ottewell, Guy, xiv

P

Palitzch, Johann, 91-92
Pallas (asteroid), 84
Paradise Lost (Milton)—poem, 134
Paradiso (Dante)—poem, 124
Paths of the Planets, The (Tricker), 77
Pavo constellation, 107
Pawnee tribe poetry, 159
Perseid meteor showers, 95
Perseus constellation, 7
Persian people, 9, 18, 20

Peru, 19, 104
Philolaus (astronomer), 69
Phoenician sailors, 101-102, 103
Piazzi, Giuseppe, 83
Pisces (Fishes) constellation, 14, 20
Piscis Austrinus (Southern Fish) constellation, 20
Planets, 60-65. *See also specific planet*
 Brahe and the, 72
 Copernicus and the, 67-78
 distances from the Sun of, 82-85
 Earth-centered system and, 66
 horizontal motion of, 26
 Kepler and the, 73-77, 85-87
 symbol for the, astronomical, 176
 technical data on, 167-170
Platonic solids theory, 74-76, 85-87
Pleiades asterism, 17
Plough asterism, 2-3, 6, 11
Pluto, 68, 84, 85
Poetry, hymns, and the stars, 117. *See also specific hymn; specific poem*
Pointers (Southern), 107-108
Polaris (star), 5, 6-7
Pollux (star), 18
Polo, Marco, 107
Private Universe, A xi
Procyon (star), 79
Proxima Centauri (star), 108
Psalm of David, 121
Ptolemy of Alexandria
 Earth-centered astronomy and, 78
 Hadar star and, 108
 poetry of, 124
 spherical nature of Earth and, 55
 star catalogue of, 79-80
Publications and materials, useful, 179-181
Puppis constellation, 106
Purgatory (Dante), 104-105
Pyramid of Khufu, Great, 38
Pyramids and altitude measurement, 38
Pythagoras, 69
Pythagorean people, 55
Pyxis constellation, 106

Q

Quadrantids meteor showers, 96

R

Radiant and meteor flashes, 93, 95
Ram (Aries) constellation, 17
Regimiento de Navegacion (Medina), 33
Regulus (star), 18

Revolving Heavens (Waterfield), ix
Richaud, Father, 108
Rigil (Rigel) Kentauris (star), 108
Rime of the Ancient Mariner (Coleridge)—poem, 46, 102, 139
Roman people, 8, 18, 19
Romeo and Juliet (Shakespeare)—poem, 129
Rubaiyat (Khayyam)—poem, 124
Rudolf II (Emperor), 73, 74

S

Sagittarius (Archer) constellation, 14, 20, 111
Saturn, 64, 66, 68, 77
Scales (Libra) constellation, 19
Schneps, Matthew, xi
Science Teaching through its Astronomical Roots (STAR), xi
Scorpion (Scorpius) constellation, 19, 111
Seasons and the sun, 23-28
Secret of the Universe, The (Duncan), 85
Shadows and the sun, 28-29, 37-41
Shapiro, Irwin, xi
Shelton, Ian, 114
Shooting stars, 93-96
Sidereal period, 2, 167, 170
Sing-Song (Rossetti)—poem, 147
Sirius (star), 79, 107
Sir Patrick Spens—poem, 159
61 Cygni (star), 71
Solstice in Northern Hemisphere, 16
Song for St. Cecilia's Day, A (Dryden)—poem, 135-136
Song of Hiawatha, The (Longfellow)—poem, 143
Song of the Sky Loom (Tewa Tribe), 158
Sonnet No. 116 (Shakespeare)—poem, 129
South celestial pole, 1
Southern Celestial Clock, 103-104
Southern Cross constellation, 103-106, 108
Southern Fish (Piscis Austrinus) constellation, 20
Southern Hemisphere, 101
 borderline zones in, 27-28
 geometrical symmetry between Northern and, 115-116
 mapping stars in, 108-111
 Moon/Sun in, 102-103, 111-112
 Pointer stars in, 107-108
 Southern Cross constellation in, 103-106
 Supernova 1987a and, 112-115
 winter/spring elongations of Mercury in, 161-162

South pole, 25, 26
Spica (star), 19
STAR. See Science Teaching through its Astronomical Roots
Starlight Night, The (Hopkins)—poem, 149
Star Morals (Nietzsche)—poem, 150
Star Names: Their Lore and Meaning (Allen), 105
Stars. *See also Constellations; Southern Hemisphere; specific stars; Zodiacal constellations*
  brightest, 172
  celestial sphere and, 1
  circumpolar, 1, 3, 4-5, 9-10
  geometrical symmetry and, 115-116
  horizontal motion of, 26
  mapping/graphing, 3-5, 15-16, 21-22, 109-111, 177-178
  nearest, 173
  occultation of, 47
  "proper" motions of, 79-80
  shooting, 93-96
  underground viewing of, 39
Stars in Song and Legend (Porter), 6
Stars (de la Mare)—poem, 152
Star-Splitter (Frost)—poem, 154
Star-Talk (Graves)—poem, 155
Steiner, Rudolf, xiii, 151
Stella, To (Shelley)—poem, 123
Sun
  altitude of the, measuring, 37
  arc movements of the, 45
  Brahe and the, 72
  comet tails and the, 92
  Copernicus and the, 67-71, 74, 78
  distances of planets from the, 168
  eclipses of the, 56-59, 165
  Kepler and the, 73-74
  latitude/longitude measurements and the, 32-34
  modern astronomy and the, 80
  moon phases and the, 42-43
  observation of from moon, 50
  seasons and the, 23-28
  shadows and the, 37-41
  Southern Hemisphere and the, 102-103, 111
  sundial construction and the, 34-36
  symbol for the, astronomical, 176
  time and the, 29-32
Sundial construction, 34-36
Sundials: Their Theory and Construction (Waugh), 29, 36
Superior planets, 60, 63-64, 66-67, 163-165
Supernova 1987a, 112-115
Swan (Cygnus) constellation, 8
Symbols, astronomical, 175-176
Synodic period, 49, 65, 167
Syrian people, 20

T

Tarantula Nebula, 114
Task, The (Cowper)—poem, 137
Taurus (Bull) constellation, 17, 111
Tempel-Tuttle comet, 94
Temper, The (Herbert)-poem, 132
Teutonic nations, Great Bear constellation and, 7
Thales (philosopher), 38
Thuban (star), 9, 38-39
Tides and the moon, 48-49
Timaeus (Plato), 122-123
Time, star movements and, 9-11, 29-32
Time standards, 171
Titius-Bode Law, 82-85
Titius-Bode Law of Planetary Distances: Its History and Theory (Nieto), 85
To Morning (Blake)—poem, 139
To Night (Shelley)—poem, 142
To the Evening Star (Blake)—poem, 138
To the Moon (Shelley)—poem, 141
Triangles and altitude measurement, 38
Troilus and Cressida (Shakespeare)—poem, 128
Tropic of Cancer, 27
Tropic of Capricorn, 27
Turanian people, 18
Turkish people, 20
Twins (Gemini) constellation, 14, 18, 111, 115
Tycho's star, 8

U

Universe in the Classroom, The, xi
Uranus, 68, 83
Ursa Major (Great Bear) constellation, 2, 6-7, 116

V

van Gogh, Vincent, 150
Varahamihira (astronomer), 88
Vega (star), 9, 80
Vela constellation, 106
Velocities, planetary orbital, 169
Venus
  Earth-centered system and, 66, 67
  elongations of, 162-163
  platonic solids theory and, 86
  Sun movements and visibility of, 60-63
  synodic period and, 65
  transits across the sun by, 166
Vesta (asteroid), 84
Virgin (Virgo) constellation, 14, 19
Voyage to the Equinoctial Regions of the New Continent (Humboldt), 104

W

Waldorf schools, xiii
Wanderers (de la Mare)—poem, 152
Waning Moon, The (Bryant)—poem, 143
Waterman (Aquarius) constellation, 20, 93
Watts, Isaac, 137
When I Heard the Learn'd Astronomer (Whitman)—poem, 145
Winter Heavens (Meredith)—poem, 147
Wittenberg, Johann T., 82
Wordsworth, William, 140
Works and Days (Hesiod)—poem, 122n

Z

Zach, Baron von, 83
Zodiacal constellations, 13-22
  mythology and, 17-21
    Southern Hemisphere and, 108-110
    Sun movements and, 24-25
    symbols for, astronomical, 175

Albatross Book of Verse. Edited by Louis Untermeyer. London and Glasgow: Collins Publishers, 1960.

An Anthology of World Poetry. Edited by Mark Van Doren. London: Cassell and Company Ltd., 1939.

Ballads of a Cheechako by Robert W. Service. London: T. Fisher Unwin, 1910.

The Book of the Dead. Translated by Sir E. A. Wallis Budge. 2nd ed., revised and enlarged. New York: E. P. Dutton & Co., 1938. (Source of the illustration on p. 119).

A Book of Science Verse. Selected by W. Eastwood. London: Macmillan & Co., Ltd., 1961.

Collected Rhymes & Verses—Walter de la Mare. 3rd. ed. London: Faber and Faber, 1945.

A Collection of Riddles from Shetland. Collected by Calum I. Maclean and Stewart F. Sanderson. Reprinted from *Scottish Studies*, vol.4, part 2, pp.150–186, 1960.

Comedy of Dante Alighieri, Cantica III, Paradise. Translated by Dorothy L. Sayers and Barbara Reynolds. London: Penguin Books, 1962.

The Complete Poems of D.H. Lawrence. Collected and edited with an introduction and notes by Vivian de Sola Pinto and Warren Roberts. New York: The Viking Press, 1964.

The Complete Poems of John Keats and Percy Bysshe Shelley. New York: The Modern Library, n.d.

The Complete Poetical Works of Wordsworth. Boston: Houghton Mifflin Company, 1932.

The Cosmographia of Bernardus Silvestris. A translation with introduction and notes by Winthrop Wetherbee. New York: Columbia University Press, 1973.

First Steps in Astronomy without a Telescope by P.F. Burns. London: Ginn and Company, Ltd., n.d.

The Gay Science by Friedrich Nietzsche. Translated, with commentary by Walter Kaufmann. New York: Random House, Vintage Books, 1974.

The Great Intellectual Revolution by J.F. West. London: John Murray, 1965.

Great Writings of Goethe. Edited and with an introduction by Stephen Spender. New York: The New American Library, A Mentor Book, 1958.

Hesiod: Theogony, Works and Days and *Theognis: Elegies.* Translated and with introductions by Dorothea Wender. London: Penguin Books, 1973.

The High Firmament: A Survey of Astronomy in English Literature by A.J. Meadows. Leicester, England: Leicester University Press, 1969.

The Home Book of Modern Verse. Compiled and arranged by Burton Egbert Stevenson. 2nd edition. New York: Holt, Rinehart and Winston, 1953.

Johannes Kepler: Life and Letters by Carola Baumgardt. London: Victor Gollancz, Ltd., 1952.

Legends of the Stars by Mary Proctor. London: George G. Harrap & Co., Ltd., 1922.

The Letters of Vincent van Gogh. Selected, edited and introduced by Mark Roskill. London: Fontana/Collins, 1965.

Living the Sky: The Cosmos of the American Indian by Ray A. Williamson. Boston: Houghton Mifflin Company, 1984.

Looking for Life. Poems by Rex Raab. Sussex, England: The Lanthorn Press, n.d.

The Metaphysical Poets. Selected and edited by Helen Gardner. London: Penguin Books, 1966.

Moonstruck: An Anthology of Lunar Poetry. Selected and with an introduction by Robert Phillips. New York: The Vanguard Press, Inc., n.d.

One Day Telleth Another by Stephen A. and Margaret L. Ionides. London: Edward Arnold & Co., 1939.

The Oxford Book of English Verse: 1250–1900. Chosen and edited by Arthur Quiller-Couch. London: Oxford University Press, Clarendon Press, 1925.

The People by Mark Littmann. Salt Lake City: Hansen Planetarium, 1976.

Poems of Gerard Manley Hopkins. 3rd ed. London: Oxford University Press, 1948.

Poems of William Cullen Bryant. Oxford edition. London: Oxford University Press, 1914.

"Poetic Responses to the Copernican Revolution" by Margaret M. Byard. *Scientific American,* no. 236 (June 1977).

Robert Frost's Poems. New York: Pocket Books, Washington Square Press, 1971.

The Stars Above Us by Ernst Zinner. Translated by W.H. Johnston. London: George Allen & Unwin, Ltd., 1957.

The Stars in Our Heaven: Myths and Fables by Peter Lum. London: Thames and Hudson, n.d.

The Story of the Stars by George F. Chambers. 2nd ed. London: George Newnes, Ltd., 1896.

Timaeus and Critias by Plato. Translated, with an introduction and appendix by H.D.P. Lee. London: Penguin Books, 1965.

They Dance in the Sky: Native American Star Myths by Jean Guard Monroe and Ray A. Williamson. Boston: Houghton Mifflin Company, 1987.

The Vedic Experience: Mantramañjari. Edited and translated with introductions and notes by Raimundo Panikkar. Berkeley: University of California Press, 1977.

Verses and Meditations by Rudolf Steiner. London: Rudolf Steiner Press, 1972.

William Shakespeare: The Complete Works. Edited, with an introduction and glossary by Peter Alexander. London: Collins, 1951.

The World's Best Poems. Edited by Mark Van Doren and Garibaldi M. Lapolla. Cleveland: The World Publishing Company, 1954.

The Works of Francis Thompson. Poems: Volume II. London: Burns & Oates, Ltd., 1913.

NORMAN DAVIDSON

was born in Edinburgh, Scotland, in 1933. He was a journalist in
the U. K. for ten years, reporting and writing on social and cultural
events. Following this, he was a Waldorf school teacher in England
for sixteen years, his subjects including astronomy, geometry, history,
and literature. Currently he is Director of Teacher Training at the
Waldorf Institute of Sunbridge College, Chestnut Ridge, New York.
An amateur astronomer, he lectures widely on astronomical and
cultural topics and is the author of *Astronomy and the Imagination*
(Arkana/Penguin), of which this book is the companion. In 1987, he
was awarded an honorary LL.D. degree by International College,
Los Angeles, for his work to "forge a bridge between the sciences
and the arts" through his "pioneering efforts in astronomy" and
for his "highly commendable" work in the education of children and
of adults.